ALOHA
RODEO

ALOHA RODEO

THREE HAWAIIAN COWBOYS, THE WORLD'S GREATEST RODEO, AND A HIDDEN HISTORY OF THE AMERICAN WEST

DAVID WOLMAN

AND

JULIAN SMITH

WILLIAM MORROW

An Imprint of HarperCollins*Publishers*

HarperCollins books may be purchased for educational, business, or sales promotional use. For information, please email the Special Markets Department at SPsales@harpercollins.com.

FIRST EDITION

Designed by Fritz Metsch

Maps by Paul J. Pugliese

Library of Congress Cataloging-in-Publication Data has been applied for.

ISBN 978-0-06-283600-7

19 20 21 22 23   LSC   10 9 8 7 6 5 4 3 2 1

To Spencer, Vivian, Ivy, and Aria

CONTENTS

PART III

ALOHA
RODEO

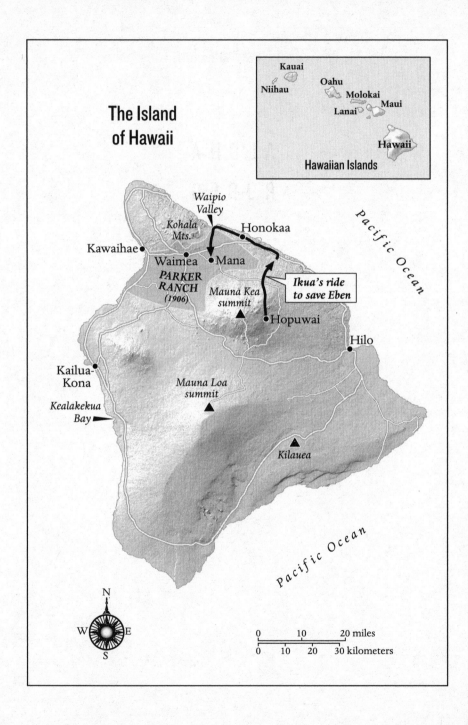

The Island
of Hawaii

Hawaiian Islands

Kauai

Niihau

Oahu

Molokai

Lanai

Maui

Hawaii

Pacific Ocean

Waipio
Valley

Kohala
Mts.

Honokaa

Kawaihae

Waimea

Mana

*Ikua's ride
to save Eben*

PARKER
RANCH
(1906)

Mauna Kea
summit

Hopuwai

Hilo

Kailua-
Kona

Mauna Loa
summit

Kealakekua
Bay

Kilauea

Pacific Ocean

N

W   E

S

0   10   20 miles

0   10   20   30 kilometers

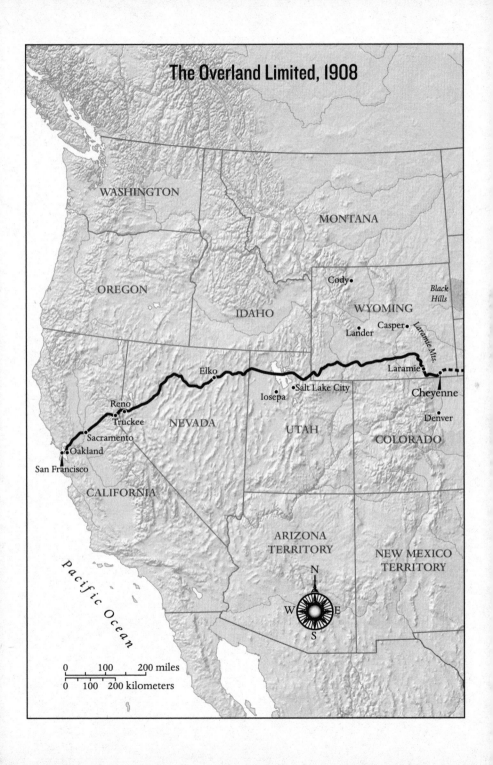

The Overland Limited, 1908

PROVING GROUND

AUGUST 21, 1908. A drizzly late-summer morning on the high plains of eastern Wyoming. The sun was just rising over Cheyenne, but hundreds of competitors and thousands of spectators were already milling about the arena on the north edge of town. They sipped home brews, chatted about the coming winter, and tried to catch a glimpse of the men the local papers had dubbed "the lithe youngsters from the far Pacific."

When Ikua Purdy and his two cousins finally entered the rodeo grounds of the bustling frontier town, the crowd eyed them with suspicion and mild amusement. Like the other wranglers, the three men wore boots, blue jeans, and spurs. But head to toe, their gear looked different: broader hat brims, smaller spurs, leather chaps, and braided rawhide lassos. Around their hats they wore strings of local wildflowers that evoked their home on the island of Hawaii.

Few people saw them as a threat. This was Wyoming, after all, home to rodeo champions and cattlemen as rugged as the landscape they worked. Still, they were clearly outsiders, like unknown drifters stepping into a dimly lit saloon.

This morning, though, they had stepped onto the biggest stage there was: Cheyenne Frontier Days. What had started as little more than an entrepreneurial whim a decade earlier had—with help from William "Buffalo Bill" Cody, Annie Oakley, Theodore Roosevelt, and countless Native Americans—ballooned into the most prestigious cultural showcase and rodeo competition on Earth. By 1908, the arrival of contestants from the South Pacific was proof that the "Daddy of 'Em All" had become the premier rodeo. Whoever triumphed here was the undisputed champion of the world. Every year so far, local boys from Wyoming had won the cattle roping competition. The Hawaiians had traveled almost four thousand miles to try to break that streak.

What the press, spectators, and other competitors didn't know, and indeed almost no one in the country did, was that ranchers in Hawaii had been breaking horses, roping wild bulls, and herding thousands of cattle before anyone in the American West. These men, like their fathers and grandfathers, made their living doing exactly what all the other contestants did: they were cowboys. *Paniolo*, in Hawaiian. Damn good ones at that.

Yet side glances and snickers were not the only challenges that Ikua Purdy, Jack Low, and Archie Kaʻauʻa had to contend with during their stay in Wyoming. A great deal rested on their shoulders. The overthrow of Hawaii's monarchy and the forced annexation of the country by the United States a decade earlier had traumatized an independent nation whose traditions dated back centuries. The young riders brought with them the pride and anxiety of an entire people reeling from a sustained attack on their cultural identity and apprehensive about their future under the rule of overlords an ocean away.

The halls of Washington echoed with debate about how best to deploy America's new military and economic might. Those who espoused empire-building were winning. At the turn of the twentieth century, America's frenzy of imperialism took the Stars and Stripes to Cuba and the Philippines, Puerto Rico, Guam, and Hawaii.

On a map, the archipelago is a tiny arcing chain of dots amid the largest expanse of blue on the planet, like a spatter of paint on a wall. But Hawaii's isolation is, paradoxically, what makes the islands' story, and that of its cowboys, one of interconnectedness. That thread connects Polynesian voyagers, Spanish conquistadores, and British seafarers bearing unexpectedly far-reaching gifts. It weaves through international trade in whale oil, sandalwood, beef, and leather goods, and extends to the birth of that most American of sports, rodeo, which at the turn of the twentieth century was spreading like prairie wildfire.

This is the story of the rise of paniolo culture in Hawaii and rodeo in America, Wyoming in particular, and the remarkable year when those worlds collided. It overturns simplistic notions of cowboys and Indians, and explores questions of identity, imperialism, and race. Most of all, though, it is a tale about people: warriors, ranchers, showmen, cowgirls, missionaries, immigrants, royalty, and the countless unnamed individuals whose lives, through the micro-accidents of history, intertwine in this little-known saga of the American West.

———

DESPITE THE MIST AND unseasonably cold wind, tens of thousands of people packed Frontier Park that August morning. One paniolo, Archie Ka'au'a, lassoed and dispatched his steer with such ease that locals did a double take. But flukes happen in rodeo. Champions are consistent. The cowboys of the Front Range of the Rockies, embarrassed by the Hawaiians' performance, were suddenly eager to put them in their place.

The next competitor, mounted on a horse he had met only days before, was Archie's cousin Ikua Purdy. While most spectators saw him as little more than a curiosity, a handful of them knew better. At rodeos in the islands, Ikua had posted times that put him in the highest echelons of the sport, and within striking distance of five-time U.S. roping champion and Wyoming native son Angus MacPhee. The small, wiry Hawaiian in the brightly colored striped shirt was the real deal: not just the best paniolo in Hawaii, but one of the best cowboys anywhere.

Ikua glanced up to see the parting clouds beyond the crowded grandstand. Then he took an extra turn of the reins around his left hand, checked that his lariat was untangled, and called out, "Steer!" The gates flew open and the animal bolted into the arena.

A moment later Ikua kicked his heels, and man and horse lunged forward as one.

PART I

I
———

HIGH STEAKS

THE FIRST CATTLE TO set foot in Hawaii didn't live to see sunset.

It was February 19, 1793, and HMS *Discovery* had arrived at the island of Hawaii after a month-long journey from what is now Southern California. Captain George Vancouver commanded the ten-gun Royal Navy ship, which was midway through a five-year expedition to explore and map the coast of North America.

Before leaving the mainland, Vancouver and his hundred-man crew had loaded ten black longhorn cattle on board. These beasts crossing the Pacific had transatlantic roots: the Spanish had brought cattle to the New World even before Hernán Cortés conquered the Aztecs in 1521. By the end of the eighteenth century, large-scale sheep and cattle ranching was entrenched throughout the territory of New Spain, especially in Alta California.

Vancouver had been dispatched to the Pacific Coast in the aftermath of a near war between Great Britain and Spain over the ownership of northwestern North America. He had orders to assert British claims and collect compensation from Spain for any seized British assets. When the *Discovery* arrived in Alta California in late 1792, a Spanish commandant presented Vancouver with the longhorns.

The animals were crammed belowdecks on the *Discovery* so tightly they could barely move. They lived ankle-deep in their own filth during the voyage, with scant portions of food and water. The wide span of their horns, which for bulls could reach six feet from tip to wicked tip, made the situation only more crowded and dangerous.

When *Discovery* dropped anchor off the northwest coast of Hawaii, the animals' situation went from bad to worse. A bull and a cow were dragged up on deck, where they were blasted by the sudden glare and heat of the tropical sun. Sailors strapped them into harnesses and lowered them over the side of the ship into narrow Polynesian canoes that bobbed in the waves.

Hawaiian paddlers pulled rhythmically through the water, ferrying their exotic cargo toward the beach. The cattle were a gift for Kamehameha, the ruler of the archipelago the British called the Sandwich Islands. Yet the animals were more than a novelty present. In the eyes of Europeans, cattle were useful to the point of being indispensable, providing meat, milk, leather, and fertilizer. On these remotest of islands, they would—and should—be welcomed, even coveted.

They were also instruments of imperialism. After the recent loss of its American colonies, mighty Great Britain was more determined than ever to spread its economic and political influence by establishing more overseas colonies. The era of an empire on which "the sun never sets" was still ahead, but

British possessions were already spread around the globe. A foothold in the middle of the Pacific would be a handsome addition to the Crown's portfolio of properties.

Giving gifts to local rulers was just good statecraft. But certain presents also served as cultural and economic tethers. Vancouver calculated that cattle would be as valuable to future British interests in Hawaii as they would be to the locals.

Unfortunately, the shock of it all proved too much for the animals, already emaciated and malnourished from their voyage. The cow died before the canoe even touched the beach, and the bull expired soon after.

It was an ignominious start. Days later, Vancouver would try again. Little did anyone know the profound impact those cattle would have on the fate of the islands, and on a future sport called rodeo.

THE ISLAND OF HAWAII covers approximately 4,000 square miles, roughly the size of Los Angeles County, and accounts for almost two-thirds of the land area of the archipelago. On the southern part of the Big Island, as it is sometimes called, Mount Kilauea continues its steady eruptions, occasionally sending lava to the sea in explosions of steam. The massive twin summits of Mauna Loa and Mauna Kea make up the island's midsection. From its underwater base to its summit, 13,802 feet above sea level, Mauna Kea is Earth's largest mountain, rising over 33,000 feet. (Everest is 29,029 feet tall.)

The slopes of Hawaii's volcanoes are not nearly as steep as jagged ranges like the Alps or the Rockies. Yet their incessant rise, lack of water, and wide temperature swings made them just as wild. To outsiders, it was an alien landscape of red-tinged cinder cones, sinuous gullies and ravines, and flows of hardened lava wending down to the sea.

One of the most isolated archipelagoes on Earth, the Hawaiian Islands are nowhere near any of the plate boundaries underlying most of the world's volcanoes. In geological parlance, Hawaii is a hot spot. Here, an extra-hot body of magma below Earth's crust pushes against the plate above, not unlike a candle held under a sheet of paper. The bulging magma presses and melts its way up to the surface and eventually breaks through. Lava piles up and gradually creates islands.

The Hawaiian hot spot doesn't move, but the Pacific Plate grinds three to four inches northwest every year. So the subterranean plume heats and pushes material through the crust at many points, as if a conveyor belt were sliding over it. The result is a chain of islands stretching northwest to southeast. Eruptions are still adding to the island of Hawaii, the youngest in the group, while older, smaller islands, now well past the plume, are eroding back into the sea.

Over time, plants, insects, and eventually animals made their way across the ocean and spread throughout the islands. Some species arrived thanks to exceptional hardiness, like the floating, saltwater-proof seeds of the palm tree. Other seeds arrived in the bellies of birds or stuck to wings and feet. Seals swam, bats flew, and insects rode trade winds. They all arrived to find an ecosystem with virtually no native predators.

As evolution ran its course, an environment emerged unlike anywhere else on the planet. A rainbow of unique species includes the pueo, an owl that nests underground, the happy-face spider, with a grin-shaped red curve on its back, and the naupaka flower, which looks like half of its white petals have been removed. According to Hawaiian legend, it was divided by parting lovers.

Other flora and fauna caught a ride with daring human mariners who set out across the Pacific some eight hundred years ago. These open-ocean voyages were an achievement with few parallels in human history. Larger than all of Earth's land-masses put together, the Pacific Ocean was the ultimate frontier. Lewis and Clark trekked and paddled over 3,700 miles across North America, roughly the same distance Christopher Columbus sailed from Portugal to the Caribbean. Polynesians, by comparison, managed to explore and colonize minuscule islands separated by as much as 5,000 miles of open ocean—without any navigational aids besides winds, currents, and stars.

Most archaeologists agree that the first people arrived on the island of Hawaii between the eleventh and the thirteenth centuries, probably from the Marquesas Islands, 2,300 miles to the south. They fished and grew crops like sweet potato, bread-fruit, and taro, a tropical plant that produces an underground stem rich in carbohydrates. The confidence, competence, and accomplishment of early settlers became central to Hawaiian society and identity.

The outside world's first recorded contact with Hawaii was Captain James Cook's arrival at Kauai in January 1778, during his third globe-spanning voyage of exploration.* The crews of the ships *Resolution* and *Discovery* found a thriving civilization of over 650,000 people. Tattooed natives lived in huts made of pili grass and raised fish in artificial ponds along the shore, cultivated extensive taro fields, and expertly navigated outrigger canoes to cross between islands.

Cook later traveled on to Hawaii. "When we first approached the coast of this island," he wrote in his journal, "we were astonished at the sight of a mountain of stupendous height, whose head was covered in snow." The Hawaiians helped the explorer and his crew resupply their ships and traded provisions for European goods. Dutifully following British custom, Cook named the archipelago after his patron John Montagu, 4th Earl of Sandwich.

In the late eighteenth century, the Western world's major powers—England, France, Spain—were snapping up lands to enrich themselves and gain strategic advantage over one another. Cook's eleven years of exploration swung the territorial land grab in Britain's favor and altered the geopolitical fate of much of the globe. At the same time, the tools, animals, and diseases he and his men brought to foreign lands dramatically affected the heath, culture, and ecology of the places he "discovered."

Just months before first sighting Hawaii, Cook visited Tahiti, where he had been on both of his previous journeys. This time he delivered cattle to the Tahitians and found the natives

---

* According to Hawaiian oral traditions, Spanish, and possibly Dutch, travelers reached Hawaii before Cook.

receptive to the "civilizing influence" of these animals. He warned the local chiefs not to kill them off too fast, and left feeling confident that his gift would be of great benefit to the islanders.

After a side trip to search for the Northwest Passage, Cook returned to Hawaii in the winter of 1778–1779. He didn't have cattle with him, but even if he had, he probably never would have had an opportunity to present them. When he and his men landed at Kealakekua Bay on the western shore of Hawaii on January 16, 1779, the Hawaiians welcomed them with honors; King Kamehameha himself draped a red cape over Cook's shoulders. Hundreds of canoes swarmed around the ships and the island's chiefs held a lavish feast. But cultural misunderstandings of some kind caused relations to sour, and on February 14, Hawaiian warriors bludgeoned Cook to death on the beach at Kealakekua. Vancouver, then a twenty-one-year-old seaman on Cook's expedition, was part of the group sent to fetch the captain's body—or at least the parts of it they could find—so that Cook could receive a proper burial at sea.

The British promptly left the islands, but the march of globalization barely slowed. In February 1793, Vancouver, now the head of his own expedition, returned to Hawaii aboard a new HMS *Discovery* (named after Cook's ship). He had intended to land at Kealakekua Bay, where Cook had died, but the winds were unfavorable. Instead, Vancouver anchored off a harbor called Kawaihae, forty miles north.

The explorer's impression of the place was not exactly romantic. "The country, in this point of view, had a very dreary aspect," he wrote, "perfectly uncultivated and nearly destitute of habitations." But he had his orders: fill in the blank spaces left in Cook's charts and restore good relations with the Sandwich Islanders.

Cattle were central to Vancouver's plan. He agreed with Cook on the economic and civilizing power of "useful" gifts and their value in linking Hawaii to the British empire's growing web of trade throughout the Pacific. These imports, Vancouver wrote, "could not fail of being highly beneficial, not only to the resident inhabitants, but also to all future visitors"— meaning, of course, Brits like him.

Hawaii was a tough environment for a cow. Temperatures could be hot and humid, and parts of the island had limited freshwater. The landscape alternated between sharp lava rocks covered with thin, nutrient-poor grasses, dry, high-altitude slopes, and muddy, dense forests. Then there were the lava flows: huge black ribbons of recently cooled and deadly sharp rock, not to mention places where fresh lava still flowed. More paved-over than pastoral, much of the terrain was about as hospitable to a grazing animal as a brick oven.

The island did at least have open grassy spaces at middle elevations, and few mammals other than pigs and dogs to compete with, so cattle would have no predators to fear.

VANCOUVER WAS UNSURE HOW he would be received. He had not forgotten how his captain was killed and dismembered fourteen years earlier, and there had been other accounts of hostility toward outsiders since then. On his first visit as expedition leader, two years before, Vancouver had found the Hawaiians uninterested in trading for any British goods except guns and ammunition, which he politely declined. This time, however, the islanders were open to trading goods such as nails and red cloth.

On the day of those first doomed cows, a fleet of canoes paddled out to the ship, led by King Kamehameha's half brother. As the king's emissary, he wanted nothing to do with the cattle at first. But after much pleading from Vancouver, he agreed to take the bizarre beasts to shore.

As Vancouver watched his bellowing gifts being lowered into the canoes, he knew the stakes were high. If things went well, the animals might help revive relations between Hawaii and Britain, the first step in drawing Hawaii into the fold of the empire. If they didn't, he could have a situation on his hands like the one that had left his predecessor dead.

After the death of the first two cattle, Vancouver's next chance came a few days later, this time at Kealakekua Bay, when he welcomed Kamehameha aboard the ship. The tall, powerful chief, described as a man who "moved in an aura of violence," wore a resplendent royal cloak covered with bright yellow feathers. Kamehameha had met Cook before he was king, and participated in the battle in which the famous explorer was killed. Now the warrior was well on his way to uniting all the Hawaiian Islands, by diplomacy and force, for the first time in history.

Upon meeting Kamehameha, the British captain was "agreeably surprised in finding that his riper years had softened that stern ferocity." As a gesture of friendship between them, Vancouver wrote, "we saluted by touching noses." Then the two men exchanged gifts, including a scarlet cloak the Hawaiian chief clearly treasured. When Kamehameha offered Vancouver hogs, vegetables, and four ceremonial helmets, the captain felt the time was right to give livestock diplomacy another try. He presented the king with two ewes, a ram, and five black cows.

Kamehameha was delighted with the animals, although, as one sailor wrote, "it took some time to quiet his fears lest they should bite him." Vancouver noted with satisfaction that the king took a rope in hand and helped secure the animals in the canoes himself. Finally free of their cramped quarters, the cattle dashed around the beach like they were calves again. A large crowd gathered to see the strange creatures. Many found them terrifying. "Thousands ran for the Sea and plunged in; every Cocoa Nut Tree was full in a moment; some jumped down precipices, others scrambled up rocks and houses."

The locals' reaction was not surprising, wrote Archibald Menzies, the *Discovery*'s botanist and surgeon, "as they were the first animals of the kind they had ever seen prancing about their country in a state so lively and vigorous." Hawaiians dubbed the cows *pua'a pipi*, or "beef pigs," since hogs were the only animals they knew that even came close.

Foreigners' accounts of these events need to be read with a critical eye. Their chronicles inevitably blend an attempt to tell what happened with considerable racial stereotyping and often total ignorance of the culture they were observing. Still, the accounts provide at least a sense of how shocked the Hawaiians were to see longhorns storming up and down the beach.

The moment those four cows hobbled onto the sand at Kealakekua was a turning point in Hawaiian history. After the exchange, Kamehameha opened the islands to the British

Navy, no longer demanding payment for safe passage. In the decades to come, cattle and cattle products would tie Hawaii into the global economy as much as other major commodities like sandalwood and sugar. And Spanish longhorns from the West Coast became one of the first links in a chain of commercial, cultural, and political influence drawing Hawaii steadily toward the United States.

Vancouver returned to Hawaii again in 1794 with three more bulls and two cows. He learned that soon after he had left the previous year, one of the animals had given birth. The Hawaiians were so elated that they immediately bundled the calf onto a man's back to carry it across the island to show the native governor in Hilo. The journey took several days, during which the Hawaiians fed the calf fish and water. "With this unnatural food the animal has been reared without the least aid from its mother," Menzies wrote, "and they assured us that it was at this time very fat and doing well."

Keen to protect his investment and boost the animals' chances of survival, Vancouver had requested that Kamehameha forbid anyone from killing the cattle until their numbers had grown. The British captain had seen sophisticated ranching operations in Spanish California, and he knew that the cattle needed royal protection until there were enough of them for a self-sustaining population.

Kamehameha agreed and imposed a *kapu*, or royal edict, forbidding anyone from killing or even hurting any cattle. Defying a kapu was punishable by death. For the sea-weary bovines, this meant they were free to wander, eat, mate, and enjoy their island home. The king also ordered a paddock built on a lush slope with easy access to spring water near modern-day Kailua-Kona. The stone enclosure was roughly five hundred acres and had walls nearly eight feet tall. (Parts of it are still there today.) Penning the longhorns was as much to protect locals from the cattle as the reverse: bulls could grow to weigh 1,500 pounds, and their deadly horns could gut a man as effectively as any spear.

The immediate goal of keeping the animals alive was to give them time to reproduce, which they did, in huge numbers, and soon there was no need to keep them penned. But the kapu also served to elevate the cattle's status. They became "the king's cattle," and centuries later, even when it became clear that the animals were agents of ecological destruction, few people ever thought of them as noxious invaders, much less tools of colonialism.

Fierce and fearless, wild cattle soon overran every island where they were introduced. In 1806, an American ship captain noted longhorns on Maui digging up gardens and destroying patches of sugarcane with their horns. One bull that charged people regularly "appeared to have a disposition to do all the mischief he could, so much so that he was a pretty unwelcome guest among them."

As Hawaiians struggled with marauding cattle, trade with the outside world was expanding quickly. Seven species of sandalwood grew in the islands, and Hawaiians used the fragrant wood to scent their homes and kill lice. Soon after the turn of the nineteenth century, American traders found that sandalwood fetched high prices in China, where it was used for incense, carving, and traditional medicine. For almost two decades, sandalwood dominated the islands' economy. Chiefs forced common people to collect sandalwood instead of fishing and tending to their farms, leading to two major famines.

But the sandalwood industry collapsed by 1830, due to foreign competition and, more so, to the fact that the trees had all been cut down. Trade in other commodities quickly filled the void: sugar, salt, tropical fruits. Hawaii was on its way to becoming the fabled crossroads of the Pacific.

Cattle and cattle products were not yet part of that mercantile boom. In February 1811, the American ship *Tonquin* sailed to the islands. The *Tonquin* was part of John Jacob Astor's ambitious, if not quixotic, plan to establish a fur-trading empire connecting the mouth of the Columbia River with New York City, London, and Canton. The crew met the governor of the island of Hawaii and paid their respects at the beach where Cook was killed. Then they sailed to Oahu and loaded up on pigs, goats, sheep, chickens, and vegetables.

When a member of the Pacific Fur Company offered to buy two beef cows from Kamehameha, the king assigned nearly a hundred men to retrieve the animals. They surrounded the herd and drove it into an enclosure. One man roped a young cow around the neck and fastened the other end to a coconut tree.

Crew members from the *Tonquin*, worried that the animal might break free, decided to shoot the cow instead. The noise triggered a stampede, and the Hawaiians—according to the ship's crew—scrambled up trees to safety. The Americans found it impossible to catch a second cow, and eventually gave up and shot another. A few more shots with blank cartridges drove the herd back to its pasture, and the Hawaiians climbed down to the ground.

It had been less than twenty years since Vancouver first delivered cattle to the islands. Thus far their influence was anything but civilizing.

2

FERAE NATURAE

ONE OF THE MOST powerful ranching dynasties in American history began with a teenager's dreams of adventure on the high seas. John Palmer Parker was born in Newton, Massachusetts, in 1790, the redheaded son of devout Puritans. He grew up a few miles from the harbor where, just two decades earlier, American colonists had revolted against their faraway overlords.

The Parker family's roots dated back a century before independence, when his great-great-grandfather emigrated from England, and generations of Parkers were well respected in their New England community. John's father, Samuel, along with a number of cousins and siblings, served in the Revolutionary War. One of his cousins was president of the United States Branch Bank, and was described as "one of the solid men of Boston" in a listing of local bluebloods. His mother, Ann, came from an Irish family and had six children.

It was a tumultuous time in America. In 1798, citing national security, Congress passed the Alien and Sedition Acts, which increased barriers to citizenship, expanded the president's

authority to detain and deport immigrants, and grossly under-
mined freedom of the press. A screwball presidential race in
1800 ended in an electoral college tie between sitting president
John Adams and Thomas Jefferson, who eventually prevailed.

Three years later, the Louisiana Purchase extended the
country's western boundary from the Mississippi River to the
Continental Divide. With a few signatures and $15 million,
the United States added more than 800,000 square miles, from
bayous to high plains to mountains—native inhabitants be
damned. To those who had advocated for it, doubling the size of
the fledgling country wasn't opportunistic; it was divine prov-
idence. Almost a century later, this spiritual, economic, and
civilizing obligation known as Manifest Destiny would push
the United States beyond the western edge of the continent and
across the Pacific.

As a student at Framingham Academy, where the curric-
ulum was steeped in Enlightenment principles, young John
Palmer demonstrated a curiosity about the world and a particular skill in mathematics. Yet despite the excitement of life in post-
revolutionary Massachusetts, Parker saw the oceans as his ticket
to fortune. New England merchants were buzzing about the
discoveries made by explorers like James Cook and the potential business opportunities abroad as trade with "the Orient"—
spices, silk, and teas for North American furs—surged. In 1809, at
age nineteen, Parker signed on with a whaling vessel, leaving
behind the deciduous forests and harsh winters of New England
to set sail for Asia. He thought he would return to Newton in a
year or two. He never did.

Parker reached Hawaii before the end of his first year at sea.

In the early nineteenth century, explorers, traders, and whaling ships were stopping in ports like Lahaina, Honolulu, and Kawaihae with increasing frequency. Like so many before and after him, Parker was transfixed by Hawaii's beauty, climate, and hospitality. But once his ship was resupplied and loaded with sandalwood, Parker departed for Canton, where he became ensnared in the turmoil of the Napoleonic Wars. Canton was one of a number of Chinese ports the British Navy blockaded to limit trade with France, leaving American mariners like Parker no choice but to wait out the conflict. Parker was still young, and this extended stay in an alien culture helped shape a famously adaptable personality.

When the blockade ended, he sailed aboard a merchant ship on a sixteen-month voyage to California and up the Pacific Coast to the Columbia River. From there, the ship traveled to Hawaii, and this time Parker stepped ashore for good. The year was 1815. He was only twenty-five, yet within a decade he would befriend a king, marry a princess, and help transform the islands' economy, landscape, and culture.

WHEN PARKER SETTLED IN Hawaii, the wild cattle situation was completely out of control. Thousands of animals roamed wherever they pleased, with virtually no fences or stone walls to stop them. They raided agricultural plots that Hawaiians had painstakingly cleared of heavy volcanic rocks and fertilized with seaweed and manure. For foraging cattle, farm plots were a veritable buffet.

To a distant observer, the west coast of the island looked

unchanged from three decades earlier, when European explorers made their first contact: a coastline dotted with thatched roofs, fishermen working the reefs, and taro plots spread out below leafy slopes. But elsewhere, especially in the upland plateau north of Mauna Kea, cattle were creating chaos and endangering lives. Visiting foreigners noted that the animals had "resorted to the mountains, and become so wild and ferocious, that the natives are afraid to go near them."

For centuries, this part of Hawaii, known as Waimea, had been a carefully gardened landscape of green hills, fertile farms, and grasslands bordered by thick forest to the north.* Cows would change all that.

The thriving newcomers acted as if they owned the place. These were not the docile, doe-eyed animals of eastern dairy farms. Longhorns were the same breed of cattle that wranglers in Alta California would sometimes pit against grizzly bears for sport. Hawaii's cattle had quickly become shrewd survivors who hid and foraged in steep pockets of forest and remote ravines. Like mountain lions, they tended to avoid people as much as possible, except when it was time to storm a garden. If startled or threatened, they would charge and chase anyone in sight.

In the early nineteenth century, a Russian merchant sloop arrived at Kealakekua and found the area overrun with wild

---

* The eastern flank of Mauna Kea was wet and foggy. Yet in the rain shadow just a few miles west, the arid terrain was vulnerable to the impacts of trampling and grazing. In the driest months of the year, it looked like the landscape of the American Southwest, even more so after the introduction of thorny mesquite and cactus.

cattle. One of the Russian explorers wrote of a herd that came down from the mountains and "committed great ravages in the plantations in the valleys." A large group of Hawaiians was dispatched to catch the animals, or at least scare them away. The cattle killed four men before disappearing back into the hills.

The situation was similar on Oahu, Maui, and soon Kauai and Molokai, too. Fences did little to prevent what one historian dubbed "the great Cattle Menace." By 1830, there were an estimated 20,000 wild cattle on Hawaii alone. The animals made it difficult to clear and farm the land, and made it hazardous to venture into the high country. "The bullocks of the mountains were . . . very numerous and savage," wrote an American traveler in 1841, "so that traveling among the mountains was attended with great danger." Another visitor, keen to explore Mauna Kea and its surroundings, found Hawaiians were "so terrified at the idea of encountering the wild cattle, which roam in prodigious numbers through the woods, that no threats or entreaties would be likely to induce them to penetrate far [into the forest] with you." In less than a quarter of a century, Vancouver's gift had become, in the words of a British explorer, completely "*ferae naturae.*"

There were a few scattered attempts at fencing and domestication. The native governor of Hawaii ordered the construction of a stone wall nearly five miles long to prevent cattle from trampling farms. On Oahu, an enterprising Spaniard named Don Francisco de Paula Marín may have been one of the first people in the kingdom to slaughter cattle and sell the beef. (By 1828, Marín's herd was up to 1,000 animals.) A former slave from the United States was reported to have a flock of goats and a handful of dairy cows inside a round fence on a six-acre homestead near Waikiki. For the most part, though, the animals remained wild and dangerous.

When Parker settled in Hawaii, he scarcely could have known that these four-legged marauders would become his ticket to riches. But his timing was perfect. The 1820s saw a dramatic increase in the number of ships arriving in the islands, including sandalwood traders, missionaries, and whaling vessels in need of provisions. More traffic meant more connections with the outside world. With expanded personal networks, it was now possible to reach foreign markets for hide and tallow (rendered animal fat used for cooking and making soap and candles). For the monarchy, the high chiefs, and those who served them, there was value in the maddening animals—but who would go after them?

Parker was socially and politically poised to capitalize on the birth of a new industry. He was among a small group of foreigners whom Kamehameha had begun grooming as advisors to help him understand and negotiate with the outside world. These relationships would prove instrumental for the king and his successors as they navigated a growing tangle of Western ideas, languages, politics, and financial opportunities.

Unlike the Protestant missionaries who had started showing up in the islands, Parker was intent on fitting in, not changing others.* He learned to speak Hawaiian, and barely a year

---

*Missionaries also learned Hawaiian, but their ultimate purpose was always saving souls.

after he arrived, he married Kamehameha's granddaughter Rachel Kipikane. The traditional ceremony concluded with a close friend throwing a bark cloth over the couple and exclaiming *Hoaoe!* or "You are married!" Parker's ability to assimilate, while simultaneously achieving a position of status and respect in a foreign culture, wasn't something he learned at the academy in Framingham or on the high seas. It was more like a social sixth sense that a person either possessed or didn't. Parker had it.

His work ethic and bilingualism made him a valuable asset to the king, a reliable grandson with respect for Hawaiian ways and a firsthand knowledge of foreign cultures. Perhaps even more beneficial was his expertise with a musket, or Brown Bess. By 1810, Kamehameha had succeeded in taking control of all the islands of Hawaii. His success hinged in part on a technological edge: two British-built warships, one of which was a forty-ton vessel armed with cannons, and muskets in the hands of his best soldiers. Since then, the king had retained a special appreciation for firearms and, by extension, the people who could use them skillfully.

Within a decade, Parker was living with his wife and infant girl on a small coastal plot given to them by the king. He fished, grew vegetables, and ventured up into the plains of Waimea to hunt cattle. But Parker was not one to settle for bucolic serenity, and the new commercial opportunities taking shape around him were hard to miss. On the rutted track connecting the nearby port at Kawaihae to Waimea, fifteen miles away and 2,600 feet higher, Parker would have seen an almost daily procession of natives transporting sandalwood and heavy timbers of koa wood, first on their backs and later in Spanish-style oxcarts. Cattle products would soon follow.

Just before his death in 1819, Kamehameha suspended the kapu on killing cattle for himself and his inner circle. He needed the money after a number of Hawaiian chiefs had racked up debts to European and American merchants and governments. Imported alcohol only made the problem worse. As one Hawaiian historian wrote: "It is plain that rum is a poison god, and debt is a viper."

Selling off the islands' sandalwood had helped with the debts temporarily. But with that resource exhausted, the kingdom needed another revenue source. To make matters worse, more powerful countries were taking notice of the monarchy's weakened financial situation. In 1826, a group of American creditors, with the support of a U.S. naval commander, negotiated a most-favored-nation trade status between Hawaii and the United States. It was an early step in a sequence being repeated around the globe: trade and investment were used to entwine colonial powers in the political affairs of less powerful nations. Then those same powers picked from a grab bag of rationales—religion, national security, "liberating" the local population, protecting the rights of citizens abroad—to justify takeover.

In Hawaii in the 1820s, this narrative of outside influence was well under way, but most foreigners were still forbidden from cutting timber or hunting cattle. Chiefs did, however, grant permission to a handful of individuals to hunt wild cattle, or bullocks,* to supply beef for the monarchy and its fleet, and for trading with visiting ships. John Palmer Parker was first on that list.

PURSUING BULLOCKS IN THE mountains of Hawaii was about as difficult and dangerous as hunting could be. Hunters armed with black-powder muskets hiked into the forested mountains around Waimea. They crossed over onto the island's eastern flank in search of huge animals with surprising speed and horns like spears. The bullocks also had an instinct for revenge. As one contemporary writer put it, if a hunter missed his first shot, the longhorns "invariably pursued their destroyers with a kind of furious madness."

Bullock hunters were generally reclusive, unpolished, and proudly independent, content to live and work far from other people. Theirs was an unforgiving profession that required a temperament as tough as koa wood. Starting with strong coffee before sunup at a backcountry campsite, a hunter began each day knowing it could bring capricious weather, riding accidents, and face-to-face encounters with half-ton creatures in treacherous terrain. A musket was the bullock hunter's essential tool, but he also caught the animals in carefully camouflaged pits, sometimes using natural holes created by collapsed lava tubes. A trapped bullock was much easier to

---

*Today *bullock* refers to a castrated bull, aka a steer, or sometimes just a young uncastrated bull. But at the time it referred to wild cattle of either sex.

shoot, but God help the man who slipped and fell in on top of it.

On Hawaii, hunters butchered animals where they fell, sometimes leaving all but the hide. Other hunters packed slabs of beef into casks of salt that native Hawaiians had hauled up-hill from the coast. Laborers then carried the casks and stiff, sun-dried hides back down to the port at Kawaihae.

Parker, the starchy New Englander turned mariner, re-invented himself as a bullock hunter in the Hawaiian wilder-ness. He roamed the mountains with a pack of trained dogs and carried gunpowder in hollowed-out bull horns. He grew to know all the shortcuts, hideouts, and secret springs of Ha-waii's mountainous interior. A crack shot, he would later claim to have killed some 1,200 animals.

For all of Parker's prowess, Hawaii's most famous bullock hunter, and the man who epitomized the type of personality drawn to the work, was an Irishman named Jack Purdy. In the early nineteenth century, Purdy fled his childhood home and found work on a whaler sailing for the Pacific. He arrived in Hawaii in 1834 and took up hunting. He built a stone house out-side Waimea that looked more suited to rural Ireland than the tropics. Compared to Parker, Purdy led a hard-charging, hard-drinking life; he once gave away an acre of land in exchange for a glass of wine. Still, he was an ace rider and shooter, and in the eyes of his contemporaries a bullock hunter without peer.

One other well-known hunter was Ned Gurney, an English-man who had escaped from the prison settlement at Botany Bay, Australia. Gurney is remembered, unfairly, for his involvement in a mysterious death in the backcountry of Hawaii. In 1834, the famed Scottish naturalist David Douglas was on a plant-collecting expedition on Mauna Kea, when he stumbled upon Gurney's grass-thatched hut and mountainside homestead. The two men shared breakfast, and then Douglas headed back out onto the trail connecting Waimea to Hilo.

Not long after Douglas's departure, however, natives found his body in a pit with a live bullock. The Scotsman had been gored and trampled almost beyond recognition. When the men told Gurney, he hurried to the spot and shot the animal so he could recover Douglas's body. Then he paid local islanders to carry the corpse to Hilo, and followed soon after to tell the authorities what had happened.

Unfortunately for Gurney, rumors circulated that the men had gotten into an argument and that Gurney had killed his guest. He was a Botany Bay man, after all, even if the crime that had him sent there from England was stealing two shillings' worth of lead. The murder accusation followed Gurney for the rest of his life. A missionary tending to him on his deathbed recalled later that Gurney raved about how he hadn't killed Douglas. Even the man of God was disinclined to believe him, saying that "wildly protested" innocence could only mean guilt.

IF HAWAII HAD A Deadwood, it was Waimea. In 1830, the island governor moved to this misty valley town tucked between the Kohala Mountains and Mauna Kea to oversee bullock hunting and trade on behalf of Kamehameha III.* He ordered convicts to build a road up from the docks at Kawaihae. Soon the winding, sun-blasted route was full of flatbed carts carrying thousands of cowhides and barrels of salted beef, lumber, *pa'i'ai* (pounded taro), and New England rum. The Kawaihae–Waimea road was only about thirteen miles long, but in local terms it was a superhighway.

American and British mariners who had had it with the sea, pioneering Chinese merchants, escaped convicts, and Hawaiian entrepreneurs all began settling in and around Waimea, drawn by opportunity in the cattle business. A visitor in the mid-nineteenth century would have found a town of more than a thousand residents with a tannery, a rendering plant, a mission school, saloons, and livestock so abundant that one local called Waimea a "cattle pen."

Residents rolling into town after days or weeks on the mountain had plenty of chances to spend their earnings on alcohol, opium, and women. In 1864, a British explorer said Waimea had been settled by the "riff-raff of the Pacific," men who "lived infamous lives, and added their own to the indigenous vices of the islands, turning the district into a perfect sink of iniquity."

When missionaries arrived, the pious newcomers from New England saw Waimea's fortune-seekers as "moral degenerates, interlopers, and political schemers." (One missionary witnessed a drunken brawl that ended with a man biting off

---

*When Kamehameha the Great died in 1919, he was succeeded by his sons Liholiho (Kamehameha II) and later Kauikeaouli (Kamehameha III).

another man's ear.) No one fit these unflattering labels more than the freelance hunters who came into town stinking of blood and leather.

The men who were attracted to occupations like sawyer and bullock hunter were an upland version of the intemperate whalers stopping over in towns like Lahaina, wild in all the ways that missionaries weren't. Lahaina, Honolulu, and other port towns had to contend frequently with rowdies, foreign sailors eager to meet women and drink themselves legless. When a Lahaina missionary lobbied the monarchy's representatives on Maui to forbid Hawaiian women from visiting whaling vessels, armed sailors showed up at his house one night to express their disagreement. The crew of a ship anchored in the harbor even fired a cannon at his house before heading out to sea to resume their slaughter of whales.

Lahaina's issues with vice finally drew the attention of the king himself. Kamehameha III ordered the construction of a building where sailors could buy goods and seek medical care. The Seamen's Hospital was meant to serve another purpose as well: to keep all the drinking, drugs, and sex hidden from the missionaries, whose presence had been sanctioned and even encouraged by the monarchy. By all accounts, this attempt to confine the town's degeneracy to one building was wholly unsuccessful. Grog and its related extracurriculars could not be repressed.

Parker steered clear of these dens of depravity, focusing his efforts on earning money instead of spending it. He partnered with another Boston-born entrepreneur, William French, who had royal approval to operate a ranch and open a trading outpost in Waimea. French, Parker, and other newcomers were betting that cattle would be Hawaii's next big thing.

Yet aside from livestock in a handful of small pens scattered around the islands, most cattle remained wild. Bullock hunters made money for the monarchy, but they could kill only so many animals. In the meantime, hunters were inadvertently teaching wild cattle to fear humans, which simply made them harder to hunt. To build an industry, Hawaii's upstart ranchers needed to control the cattle.

3

THE EMPIRE

THE NEW WORLD'S FIRST cowboys were called *vaqueros*, from the Spanish *vaca*, for cow, and *querer*, to love. Vaqueros wore clothes that combined practicality with ornamentation: hats with wide upturned brims, low-heeled boots with jingling metal spurs decorated with silver, and pants adorned with bright buttons up the seams. Their skills at riding, roping, and herding, combined with their distinctive look, gave them prestige among men and women; it was said a vaquero would dismount only to dance with a pretty girl.

By the early nineteenth century, it was clear that Hawaii's bullock hunters couldn't keep up with the islands' soaring cattle populations. Through increasing trade with North America, the monarchy had learned that vaqueros managed herds of tens of thousands at sprawling *ranchos* in Alta California. Here, finally, was a possible solution to Hawaii's bovine nightmare—and a potential moneymaker. In the early 1830s, Kamehameha III sent a royal decree to mission contacts in California. The king requested that vaqueros come to the islands to teach Hawaiians the basics of roping and herding. That same year, perhaps a dozen men, roughly three for each of the major islands, traveled from California to Hawaii.*

The vaqueros brought their own well-trained mustangs, which traveled in first class compared to livestock, with regular brushing, water, and fresh food. Storms aside, the most stressful part of the journey was the end. As one historian noted, "While embarkation in California meant dockside loading, the vaquero was apprehensive about casting his mount overboard in Kawaihae Bay for the swim to shore." But there was no alternative.

Customized gear was also critical, starting with a leather-covered saddle often stamped with intricate geometric or floral patterns. A vaquero's most important and treasured possession, though, was his *reata*, the root of the English word *lariat*. Braided painstakingly by hand out of four strips of carefully chosen rawhide, the lasso was usually about eighty feet long. A rider's job, and sometimes his life, depended on his proficiency with the rope. When it rained, the lariat was the first thing the vaquero protected.

Cowboys in Spanish Mexico had put their lassos to uses beyond herding cattle. During the Mexican-American War, lo-

---

*Before the first vaqueros traveled to the islands, there were at least a handful of Hawaiians in Spanish California and along the West Coast working aboard fur-trading vessels. An American traveler to San Diego in the 1830s reported "a dozen or twenty" Hawaiians working as "hide-curers, handlers, etc. They were greatly esteemed as hands for the vessels plying up and down the coast of California." It's possible that some of them were riding horses and roping cattle before Kamehameha III made his request for vaquero tutors, in which case they may be considered the first Hawaiian cowboys.

cal ranchers pressed into fighting employed them as weapons against American troops; dragging a man to death didn't cost any bullets. According to one story from the Mexican Revolution, a soldier once roped the muzzle of a small cannon and dragged it off. Lassos also came in handy during bear hunts in California. A colorful 1855 account in *Harper's Magazine* described how Mexicans, who could "throw the lasso with the precision of the rifle ball," would corner bears and rope them around the neck and hind foot. "[A]fter tormenting the poor brute and . . . defying death in a hundred ways, the lasso is wound around a tree, the bear brought close to the trunk and either killed or kept until somewhat reconciled to imprisonment."

In 1840, a young Yale graduate named Francis Allyn Olmsted was traveling the South Pacific and, upon arriving in Waimea, noticed men dressed in ponchos, boots with "prodigiously long spurs," and pants split along the outside seam below the knee. Olmsted watched as the men corralled cattle and branded each one prior to shipment to Honolulu: "In an instant, the lasso was firmly entangled around his horns or legs, and he was thrown down and pinioned. The burning brand was then applied, and after sundry bellowings and other indications of disapprobation, the poor animal was released."

The vaqueros taught the bullock hunters that the lasso was a more effective tool than the rifle. Ranching meant careful management: organizing, moving, slaughtering, breeding. It was about fences and grass, brands and paddocks. This was how to bring the wild herds of Mauna Kea under control.

The men from California also taught the Hawaiians how

to work with the horses that had first arrived in the islands in 1803, when an American merchant ship had brought four mounts from California as gifts for Kamehameha I. This time the king's reaction was more subdued. Even if riding was faster than walking, he asked shrewdly, would the animals be worth the food, water, and care they would require?

But in the end he accepted the gifts, and within a matter of decades, horses had become an integral part of daily life and tradition throughout the islands. Hawaiians quickly took to riding, and there is mention of importing more horses to the archipelago as early as the mid-1820s. Hawaii's first horses were mustangs from the wilds of New Spain, descendants of the tough animals the conquistadors had brought to the New World in the sixteenth century. They were Arabians, probably the oldest horse breed in the world. These compact, hardy survivors could thrive in harsh landscapes—their long-distance endurance is legendary—and they had experience working with cattle that made them perfect for their new job in the islands.

Hawaiians also adopted the vaqueros' spirit of competition. During annual roundups, or rodeos, ranches in New Spain hosted matches in which vaqueros faced off in friendly contests. These games were sometimes brutal, such as grizzly roping, or races in which riders tried to grab a live rooster buried up to its neck in the ground. Others were controlled versions of tasks the vaqueros performed every day: sprinting on horseback, lassoing and tying up steers, and breaking wild horses to the saddle.

As Hawaiians became more adept with the vaqueros'

methods and tools, they absorbed many of their mentors' sensibilities about work, animal husbandry, and even style. Some of the men Olmsted observed, in fact, were likely native Hawaiians dressed in what was fast becoming standard garb for island cowboys.

Yet they also created a uniquely Hawaiian tool kit. They slimmed down the heavy, bulky Mexican saddle into the Hawaiian tree saddle, so called because it was carved from the wood of local trees, just as their ancestors had carved canoes out of koa. Local saddlemakers added a high saddle horn for dallying, or tying, the free end of a lasso. Hawaiian riders used smaller spurs than the long Mexican ones, so as not to trip on jagged lava rock.

Hawaiians took to cattle ranching with such enthusiasm and skill that soon the vaqueros had nearly put themselves and the bullock hunters out of a job. "Already the old race of Bullock catchers (a most useless set in other respects) is becoming extinct," wrote a local rancher in 1848. Eleven years later, the Honolulu papers reported that the vaqueros who had come to teach the Hawaiians "how to lasso, jerk beef and cure hides" were all but gone, either back to North America—perhaps to California to chase gold rush fortunes—or else absorbed into Hawaiian society.

In their place were Hawaiian cowboys called paniolo, a local twist on the word *español*. The legendary cattle drives of the West were still a generation away, but here on the plains of Waimea and elsewhere in the islands, paniolo were working cattle—before there was ever such a thing as an American cowboy.

BY 1835, JOHN PALMER PARKER had left the coast of Hawaii and moved to Waimea, where he worked as a bookkeeper for William French while hunting wild bullock on the side. The general store where Parker worked quickly became a nexus for local business dealings, as well as a hangout for cowboys to "talk story." A fire would have helped counter the chill of the rain and the stink of skinned carcasses and hides, as dogs and rats foraged outside among piles of discarded entrails.

While the fastidious Parker maintained an unblinking focus on his business aspirations and spiritual virtue, Jack Purdy burnished his reputation as a hunter and mountain man nonpareil, with little apparent concern for everyday comforts and money. Despite their contrasting personalities, Parker and Purdy were neighbors and friends with much in common: they both had Irish ancestry, married Hawaiian women, and lived lives that revolved around cattle.

In 1835, both men were working for French as bullock hunters. Parker's additional job as French's bookkeeper gave him a wide lens on the emerging livestock industry. He soon shared a joint lease with French to run cattle on Mauna Kea, making the two men the first private ranchers on the island. By 1851, Parker had secured more than 1,640 acres. He knew exactly what it took to create and run a successful ranch similar to those on the mainland: horses, corrals, accessible water, and ace paniolo.

Above all, though, it took land. But the Western concept of property was alien to Hawaiians. Land wasn't something human beings could own; people cared for the land, and in turn the land took care of the people. Once Kamehameha I consolidated control of the islands, he doled out parcels of varying sizes to chiefs and relatives. Everyday Hawaiians lived on and worked the land at the behest of regional chiefs, but it wasn't theirs, or even the chiefs', to buy or sell.

Parker used his royal family connections and the two-acre plot the king had given him for a wedding present as a toehold to gain further claims and leases. As the islands' cattle industry began to flourish, other entrepreneurs—almost all of them foreigners—started leasing property as well, first to secure the right to hunt wild cattle and later for grazing.

But they soon wanted more. A system of well-defined property ownership with clear boundaries was key for successful ranch operations. Without it, reasoned the enlightened outsiders, legitimate businesses would be at the mercy of the monarchy or local chiefs. Indeed, they argued, disputes over land ownership were already breaking out.

Two of these episodes grew into international incidents, and both starred the same obstinate Englishman. Richard Charlton, British consul to the Hawaiian kingdom, leased land on Oahu to raise longhorn cattle. Charlton had no qualms about shooting any local cows or goats that wandered onto his property. Yet his own animals had a tendency to venture out after dark and stray onto nearby farms. In 1829, a Hawaiian farmer had had enough of these late-night depredations and shot one of Charlton's trespassing cows.

Charlton was livid. When his appeal to the Hawaiian government to punish the cow-killer was rejected, he took matters into his own hands. With the help of an American named

John Coffin Jones, Charlton seized the Hawaiian, tied a halter around his neck, and rode off. The man ran until he collapsed, strangled by the rope, and Charlton dragged him behind his horse until a fellow islander ran up and cut the cord.

In a letter to the king, an unrepentant Charlton argued that the current land-tenure system put people's property, and even their safety, in jeopardy—especially if those people were foreigners. But the king's response showed he was more concerned with Charlton's brutality: "[I]f you judged the man guilty, you are not forthwith to punish him; wait till we have a consultation first; then, had we judged him guilty, we would have given you damages; but no, you rashly and suddenly injured the man."

Charlton's next clash nearly led to an attack on Honolulu, and briefly resulted in the cession of the Hawaiian Kingdom to Britain. In the winter of 1842, the Englishman was on the warpath again, this time over Kamehameha III's refusal to accept a claim he had made on a piece of land in Honolulu. Charlton traveled to Mexico, where he convinced British Navy officials that the monarchy was denying the queen's citizens their rights under the law. A British captain, Lord George Paulet, set sail for the islands to demand recourse. When the king denied him an audience, Paulet made it known that he was ready to fire his ship's twenty-six guns on the town.

Kamehameha III, in a now-famous letter addressed to the Hawaiian people, agreed to relinquish power—temporarily, he hoped—until the international community stepped in to right this all-too-obvious wrong. Paulet made himself and three other Britons heads of a new Hawaiian government. Within six

months, British authorities realized that Paulet had acted un-
lawfully, egged on by Charlton. The takeover was nullified,
and Hawaii was returned to the Hawaiians. Charlton lost his
government post but kept up his property fights before finally
retreating back to England in the winter of 1846.

Dubbed the Paulet Affair, the brief occupation was a stark
illustration of how vulnerable Hawaii was to the whims of im-
perial powers. It also showed how central cows had become to
the story of the islands.

HALF-MAD ENGLISHMEN WEREN'T THE only ones pressing for land
ownership reform. Parker and others worked to convince the
monarchy that it was in everybody's best interest to end the
communal approach and start nailing down private property
titles. Together with other businessmen, he made the case that
helping ranchers would also earn the kingdom money. (The
monarchy and its circle of chiefs earned hefty commissions on
every hide or cask of tallow sold.) Some missionaries even said
private land ownership would help encourage a work ethic
among a people they considered naturally lazy.

In 1840, Kamehameha III signed a new constitution, followed by a series of laws that ultimately made it possible for
anyone to own land, including foreigners. Almost overnight, a
land grab swept across the archipelago. It was one of the most
important events in Hawaiian history: a complete redefinition
of the concept of property.

Within decades, foreigners like Parker owned huge grazing
parcels and sugar plantations spread across the islands. The

fragmented remainders consisted of native farms, many of which were too small to sustain a family. In places like Waimea, native Hawaiians who had farmed communal land for generations were forced to take up a trade or leave to find work. Most Hawaiians—everyone outside the royal family or not well connected to a chief—ended up with less than 1 percent of Hawaii's land area, while the list of names for title claims read like a New England phone book: Harris, Sinclair, Bush, French, Baldwin, Chamberlin, and Parker.

The eventual takeover of the Kingdom of Hawaii resulted from a familiar array of forces: the ravages of disease, missionaries suppressing native culture, political subterfuge, and a weak military. Yet the shift to private land ownership was also a crucial event in the saga of Hawaii's stolen sovereignty.

At the same time that Hawaiians were losing control of their ancestral territories, the U.S. government was waking up to the islands' strategic and commercial value. By mid-century, the American whaling industry was the fifth largest sector of the U.S. economy. Whale oil lubricated machinery and lit lamps, and whale baleen made stiff but flexible corsets. A single ship's cargo could turn a profit of close to $1.5 million in today's dollars.

Hawaii was the ideal place to resupply during the harsh Pacific winters, and whaling ships—most from Parker's home state of Massachusetts—were stopping by the hundreds every year. Ship captains needed to refit their vessels and stock up on fresh water and salt beef. Mainland businesses required tallow and leather for products like shoes and book jackets. As a result,

Hawaii's coastal villages were replaced by commercial harbor towns whose tidy storefronts evoked their builders' New England roots.

Honolulu, the kingdom's commercial center, was inundated with sailors ready to blow off steam. In the winter of 1845–1846, Rear Admiral Samuel Francis Du Pont of the U.S. Navy received an appeal from whaling ship captains and the American consul to have a U.S. Navy warship on hand during the height of refitting season. This would improve morale and help ease tensions between sailors and locals. Du Pont agreed wholeheartedly. The request and Du Pont's response reflected an attitude that was steadily crystallizing within America's military, business community, and, increasingly, government: the more the United States ran things in Hawaii, the better it was for everyone. The monarchy wouldn't be able to maintain its grip on power in this rapidly globalizing world, so the assumption went, and the United States couldn't afford to let another power take over. Yield Hawaii and what would come next—the West Coast?

King Kamehameha III was well aware that his rule was under threat from foreign powers, and may have considered the United States to be the devil he knew. In 1854, he ordered his minister of foreign relations to look into the idea of annexation by the United States because "plans are on foot inimical [unfavorable] to the peace of Our Kingdom and the welfare of our people, and such as if carried out would be wholly subversive of Our Sovereignty, and would reduce Us to the most deplorable of all states, a state of anarchy."

On the Fourth of July that year, a parade through Honolulu showed what the islands' foreign community thought of
the idea. A chariot carried "Young America," a boy described
by a witness as "the very personification of health, strength, and
beauty." Pulled behind that chariot was "Young Hawaii," a col-
orfully decorated boat holding eight native boys eating sugarcane. The procession ended at Kawaiahaʻo Church, where the
American commissioner delivered a speech "in which it was
more than hinted that a new star was about to be added to the
glorious constellation." The prospect of cozying up with, or
even absorbing, Hawaii was greeted enthusiastically in Washington, where President Franklin Pierce and other proponents
of expansion were carrying the torch of Manifest Destiny. Plans
for an annexation treaty were being drafted in 1854, but then
were abandoned after Kamehameha III died that December.
His successor, Kamehameha IV, scuttled the negotiations.

BY THE 1860S, THE whaling boom was all but over. Whale populations had been decimated, and petroleum products and
vegetable oils had proved better and cheaper than whale oil.
Meanwhile, Hawaii's burgeoning cattle industry was primed to
expand, fueled by cheap cattle, ample labor, and an insatiable
overseas market for salted beef, hide, and tallow. In 1860, the
island of Hawaii, population under 22,000, had about 25,000
wild cattle and another 10,000 domesticated animals. Hide and
tallow became the kingdom's top export commodities.

Through all of this, John Palmer Parker was steadily amass-
ing real estate. About eight miles east of Waimea, at a site called

Mānā, Parker had built a small home out of 'ōhi'a bark and Hawaiian grasses. In the following decades, Parker Ranch endured aggressive competition, disease outbreaks, floods, droughts, earthquakes, and volcanic eruptions. But Parker and his descendants persevered, snapping up more and more land along the way. By the end of the century, Parker Ranch was one of the largest ranches anywhere, with more than 20,000 branded cattle grazing on 300,000 acres.

Parker turned Mānā into a full-fledged manor. From the outside, the building was pure New England colonial; on the inside, the walls, floors, and even the wooden nails had the reddish glow of native koa timbers. Intermixed with the saltbox buildings were traditional Hawaiian grass houses. An orchard of peach and orange trees grew alongside manicured gardens, giving the property the air of a European country estate dropped in the tropics.

Parker provided ranch employees with denim work clothes but wore Hawaiian-style clothing himself, usually a *malo*, or loincloth. Native Hawaiian was the language of choice, the only exceptions being the children's English lessons or when foreigners visited. Guests dined and enjoyed music and dance while seated on the floor, as Hawaiian chiefs had done for ages. Even the beds were fitted with cloth made of flat-pounded bark instead of cotton sheets. Christian prayers were still held every day, and a loud note blown on a conch shell announced the weekly Sabbath service.*

---

*Parker's open-mindedness had its limits. When his daughter, Mary, fell in love with and married a Hawaiian man, he cast her out of the family.

Riders approaching Mānā would sometimes report seeing the *wahine koa*, the ghostly shape of a woman that paniolo claimed to see in the mists and rains as they crossed the
undulating pastures. A visitor in 1857 experienced a royal welcome, with dozens of native Hawaiians hurrying about to greet
guests, unsaddle horses, and prepare a feast of roast beef, ba-
nanas, and strawberries. The guest described Parker as a "cosmopolitan" who "by energetic work . . . has made a considerable
fortune."

Parker had realized his vision. The young dreamer from
Massachusetts had built, hide by hide and acre by acre, an im-
mense ranching empire, where he exercised "a baronial sway
and a noble hospitality."

John Palmer Parker died in Honolulu in August 1868. He
was seventy-eight years old. His ranch had become the beating
heart of the paniolo world, and would soon give rise to some of
Hawaii's—and America's—greatest cowboys.

4

HOLY CITY OF THE COW

ON THE MORNING OF September 5, 1898, the streets of Cheyenne, Wyoming, were lined with so many people it was almost impossible to move. Ranchers, merchants, schoolmarms, hucksters, farmhands, and children of all ages had gathered to mark the start of a celebration of life and sport in the West: Cheyenne Frontier Days.

Festivities kicked off with an extravagant parade that included enough international combatants to launch a war: twenty mounted Sioux; a company of German cavalry in white uniforms; bands of Arabs, Turks, and Mexicans on horseback; a company of Cubans; and a squadron of British lancers. They were followed by fire trucks decorated with flowers, and a train of thirty weathered prairie schooners.

Two men sat in an open carriage at the head of the convoy. One was a prominent rancher and surveyor named William Richards, who would become Wyoming's fourth governor.*

---

*Richards would be remembered for a pardon he granted to a convicted horse rustler "so that he may have the chance to become an upstanding

But the audience had come to see the other man, a distinguished gentleman whose long white hair fell over the collar of his fringed buckskin jacket. To the *Daily Sun-Leader*, the fifty-two-year-old cowboy was "handsome as a picture, bold as a lion, chivalrous to a fault, he is the beau ideal of the public, a human poem, a breathing statue, an animated painting."

His name was William Frederick "Buffalo Bill" Cody, and he may well have been the most famous person on the planet.

That day, Buffalo Bill's Wild West was the opening act to Cheyenne Frontier Days, adding the prestige of Cody's stardom to the upstart rodeo. First, spectators watched Cossacks, cavalrymen, and cowboys gallop around the prairie north of the Capitol Building. They witnessed a mock Pony Express ride, a pretend buffalo hunt, and formation riding by the 6th U.S. Cavalry. The soldiers also reenacted Cody's personal, albeit embroidered, exploits as a scout and soldier. A band filled in gaps in the action and an orator on a raised platform narrated everything at top volume. The audience, stirred by the action and military prowess on display, was primed for the rodeo competition that followed.

Buffalo Bill's Wild West and Frontier Days delivered grand entertainment the likes of which few, if any, had ever seen. For the residents of a town that had been little more than a way station for travelers headed to California and Oregon, Cheyenne suddenly felt like the center of the West.

----

citizen and possibly encourage his associates to do the same." The rustler's name was Robert Leroy Parker, alias George "Butch" Cassidy.

SOME THIRTY YEARS EARLIER, on November 13, 1867, the first passenger train arrived in Cheyenne with a screech of brakes and hiss of steam. The din heralded the start of a new era, a future of connectedness and commerce. "No use of talking," said one onlooker. "It beats the world," said another.

The settlement's name came from the tribe that had once ruled the high broad plains east of the Laramie Mountains. Here, windswept steppes and grasslands inspired a U.S. Army surveyor to coin the term Great American Desert and dismiss the entire region as "almost wholly unfit for cultivation." The area was fit for wildlife, though. Tens of millions of bison roamed and sculpted the landscape, and had so for millennia, trampling and eating their way across hundreds of miles of grassland every year.

The western reaches of the Great Plains were in fact suitable for cultivation, once farmers figured out how to tap the enormous Ogallala Aquifer for irrigation. Before then, however, settlers passed through by the thousands: pioneers headed to Oregon, fur traders eyeing the Rockies, gold seekers dreaming of California. Those who stayed lived the hardscrabble life of homesteaders in an unforgiving land of sagebrush and sandstorms, brutal sun and ice-choked rivers, a place as uninviting as it was monotonous. An early traveler described a "gray, sage-covered plain" that "with its yellow, withered grass gave a cheerless picture, made still more so by the numerous human graves."

Resident Native American tribes—Shoshone, Crow, Sioux,

Arapaho, and Cheyenne—fought a losing battle against white settlers, soldiers, and disease. By the mid-1800s, indigenous populations had plummeted by up to 90 percent since the arrival of Columbus at the end of the fifteenth century.

When California governor Leland Stanford hammered home a ceremonial golden spike at Promontory Point, Utah, on May 10, 1869, the moment commemorated a staggering engineering achievement. Completing the Transcontinental Railroad reduced what had been a six-month cross-country journey to a six-day trip. At the same time, it symbolized the stitching together of a nation recently torn apart by civil war.

In the years leading up to the golden spike, workers had raced to lay tracks from east and west at speeds of up to ten miles a day. Starting in Council Bluffs, Iowa, three months after Lincoln's assassination and the end of the Civil War, the Union Pacific Railroad snaked west across the Nebraska plains and entered southern Wyoming in late 1867. At the head of the tracks was a transient community of railroad workers, support crews, prostitutes, and hangers-on. Hell on Wheels, as the traveling town came to be known, left a ribbon of steel and a trail of mayhem across the country.

Thousands of people arrived in Cheyenne in advance of those who were laying the track, living in dugouts, tents, covered wagons, and shacks. Hell on Wheels spent six months there, longer than in most towns, before pushing farther west in January 1868. In its wake was a city whose "wickedness [was] unimaginable and appalling," wrote one Episcopal reverend. It was full of "gamblers of all shades, and roughs, and troops of lewd women, and bull-whackers [and] almost every other house is a drinking saloon, gambling house, restaurant, dance hall or bawdy." Saloons in Cheyenne were said to outnumber other businesses three to one. "Every man slept with from one to a half-dozen revolvers under his pillow," reported one visitor, "for depredations of every character could be expected at any hour, day or night."

Cheyenne grew into a buzzing, boisterous frontier town so quickly it became known as the "Magic City of the Plains." Residents organized a city government, opened hundreds of stores and saloons, and set up a newspaper and a post office. Frontier opportunities drew engineers, lawyers, and businessmen along with Native Americans, Chinese laborers, and soldiers fresh from the Civil War.

The city's police officers were overwhelmed. Cheyenne's first mayor levied a $10 fine on anyone who fired a gun within city limits, whether they hit someone or not. He tacked on an additional 25 cents to each fine "to cover the expense of stimulants necessary to efficient administration of justice." With law enforcement shorthanded (or drunk), citizens felt the need to form a vigilance committee to keep the peace. They hung or shot the occasional desperado, and turned a log cabin into a jail for vagrants and petty criminals. When the building filled up, each occupant was taken out one at a time and told to leave town. Anyone who didn't move fast enough was urged along by six-guns fired at his feet.

The frenzy diminished when the railroad moved on, and Cheyenne's population dropped from about 10,000 to 1,500. But those who remained were determined to turn Cheyenne into a real city. On July 25, 1868, the Wyoming Territory was formed out of a geographical gumbo: portions of the Utah, Dakota, and Idaho Territories, the land had been previously claimed by Great Britain, France, Spain, Mexico, and Texas, and was home to Native Americans for thousands of years before that.

The sunshine and dry air at 6,000 feet were thought to be good for people with asthma and tuberculosis, attracting patients like the famous gambler and gunfighter Doc Holliday. Other Wild West luminaries also passed through Cheyenne in her early years, including Calamity Jane, who was arrested in town twice, and Wild Bill Hickok, who played cards at the Gold Room and was married at the First Methodist Church, five months before he was murdered during a card game in Deadwood, South Dakota. Cody was there too, in 1870, and noted with approval "abundant opportunities for entertainment" like roulette and horse racing.

AS PIONEERS BEGAN SETTING down roots in the hard soil in and around Cheyenne, a handful of locals started dreaming big. Aside from Fort D. A. Russell, a U.S. Army base on the edge of town, and through traffic to the gold fields of the Black Hills, the local economy was anemic. Cheyenne had no mining, little timber, and sparse agriculture. In contrast, Denver, just a hundred miles south, was a thriving mining town: between 1870 and 1880, its population shot from about 5,000 to 36,000 people.

What Cheyenne did have was access to millions of acres of prairie, a virtual sea of grass open for grazing. Moreover, the bison that Lewis and Clark had described as "so numerous [they] darkened the whole plains" were well on their way to extermination. Farmers and ranchers killed bison for meat and to clear land for livestock and crops; tourists took potshots from moving trains; and soldiers killed bison to drive out the Native American tribes who depended on them for food and hides.

Most of the herds fell to the rifles of professional buffalo hunters. A single rifleman armed with one of the newest breech-loading long-range rifles made by Sharps or Remington could drop more than 100 animals in an hour and thousands in a single season. One hunter killed 1,142 bison in six weeks. Hunters often took only the animal's tongue, if that, and left the rest to rot.

By the 1870s, the "hunt" had become an all-out slaughter. In 1873 alone, the Atchison, Topeka and Santa Fe Railway reported shipping 250,000 buffalo robes, 1 million pounds of meat, and 2.7 million pounds of bones, to be processed into fertilizer in the East. In the words of one witness:

> Could the southern buffalo range have been roofed over at that time it would have made one vast charnel-house. Putrifying carcasses, many of them with the hide still on, lay thickly scattered over thousands of square miles of the level prairie, poisoning the air and water and offending the sight. The remaining herds had become mere scattered bands, harried and driven hither and thither by the hunters, who now swarmed almost as thickly as the buffaloes.

The last shipment of buffalo robes went out from Dickinson, Dakota Territory, in 1884. Herds that once took six days to pass through were down to fewer than 500 animals.

In the meantime, the vast rangelands of Texas and Oklahoma were overflowing with longhorns. Descendants of animals first brought from Spain, these tough long-legged beasts
could, as one historian put it, "walk to markets thousands of
miles away, through swamps and deserts, through droughts
sent by the devil himself." Five hundred miles to the north,
Cheyenne had both the sea of grass and the railway links—a
combination even Denver couldn't claim. All an enterprising
rancher needed to do was get the cattle to Wyoming.

The first longhorn cattle drives left Texas in the late 1860s.
Every summer, men on horseback guided tens of thousands of
animals north. Like paniolo in Hawaii, these cowboys were
professional descendants of vaqueros. They were honest men
and escaped criminals, experienced Civil War soldiers, former
slaves, and locals with nothing on their résumé besides riding
and roping. Some came from the East, others from abroad.
They faced biblical weather, armed conflict with Native Americans, and stampedes of half-ton animals with deadly horns, sub-
sisting for weeks on coffee, biscuits, beans, and the occasional
"slow elk," or unclaimed cow.

Men working the cattle drives had a reputation for independence, wildness, and a particular moral code. As one Cheyenne
newspaper put it:

> You find in them a strange mixture of good nature and
> recklessness. You are as safe with them on the plains as
> with any class of men, so long as you do not impose on
> them. They will even deny themselves for your com-

fort, and imperil their lives for your safety. But impose upon them, or arouse their ire, and your life is of no more value in their esteem than that of a coyote. Morally, as a class, they are foulmouthed, blasphemous, drunken, lecherous, utterly corrupt. Usually harmless on the plains when sober, they are dreaded in towns.

They did hard work for little pay, often for rich absentee landlords they never met. It was a job with countless ways to break a man, from dehydration to drowning, scalping to snake bite, trampling to tuberculosis. Yet to many, these challenges only added to the allure of running cattle, and helped shape the image of the American cowboy that would capture the imagination of the country and the world.

IF YOU HAD THE audacity and the manpower, there was money to be made in the Wyoming Territory. Once a cattle drive reached the northern plains, the Texas longhorns fattened up quickly on nutritious grasses. In the spring and fall, they were rounded up, sorted, branded, and loaded onto trains to distant markets. In 1865, cattle worth $4 a head in Texas could fetch ten times that in the Northeast. Wyoming ranchers who spent $1.50 to raise a steer could sell it for up to $60.

Cheyenne, at the intersection of trails and rails, became the center of a cattle boom that spanned Montana, Nebraska, Colorado, and Kansas. The industry fed a national appetite for meat that astonished Europeans. When the English novelist Anthony

Trollope visited the United States in the mid-nineteenth century, he estimated that Americans ate twice as much beef as the English, and noted how the typical American child was "very particular that his beefsteak at breakfast shall be hot."

A financial frenzy ensued, as investors from the East and Europe read books like James Brisbin's *The Beef Bonanza; or, How to Get Rich on the Plains* and bought up ranchlands wherever they could. "There is not the slightest amount of uncertainty in cattle raising," proclaimed the German author of *Cattle-Raising on the Plains of North America*, predicting guaranteed profits of 156 percent over five years.

By 1885, the Wyoming Territory was home to as many as two million cattle. The Magic City of the Plains earned a new nickname, the "Holy City of the Cow," and Cheyenne became by some estimates the wealthiest city its size in the world. It was one of the first cities in the United States to have electric streetlights, and boasted a working telephone exchange five years after Alexander Graham Bell patented the invention. Opulent houses complete with crystal chandeliers and hand-carved woodwork lined the downtown streets. There was even a polo field and a thousand-seat opera house.

Yet the gilded cattle town retained its rough edges. The wide streets still weren't paved, and horse thieves were occasionally found hanging from the branches of a cottonwood. Not that the line between rich and bawdy was ever entirely clear: opposite the opera house and the Baptist church stood the two-story "House of Mirrors," the most exclusive brothel in the state. Its guest list overlapped with that of the Cheyenne

Club, a place for wealthy cattle barons to talk business over fine whiskey and Havana cigars. Above the main bar hung a painting of a prize bull by the famed Dutch artist Paulus Potter—with a bullet hole in it.

BUT BOOMS DON'T LAST. Thanks to bad luck, poor decisions, and changing demographics, Cheyenne's financial bust was swift. For one thing, the city was too dependent on a single commodity. Then Mother Nature stepped in, as if hell-bent on killing cattle.

First, a scorching summer in 1886 left little grass available on rangelands that were already overgrazed. An army commander posted in northeastern Wyoming wrote, "The country is full of Texas cattle and there is not a blade of grass within 15 miles." Then November rains soaked fields, which became sheets of ice during one of the most horrific winters on record. Deep snows and arctic temperatures started early and rarely abated. Even the piercing winds weren't strong enough to uncover the grass and water the cattle needed to survive. Cows starved or froze to death by the thousands, with dead cattle piling up against newly built barbed wire fences.

"We had wood and warmth, and grub to eat, but our hearts went out to the bawling, drifting and starving cattle," recalled one cowboy. "Both day and night the cries for food were heard, but we were powerless to help them."

No one who rode the range in the spring of 1887 ever forgot the sight of gullies filled with the dead. Along one fence in North Texas, cowboys skinned 250 carcasses per mile for thirty-five miles. The emaciated animals that survived stood in a daze, their ears still frozen, too feeble to walk. The "Big Die-Up" wiped out entire herds.

Yet the death knell for the giant ranches—and Cheyenne's economic heyday—was the unstoppable influx of new settlers claiming land. From 1880 to 1890, Wyoming's population grew by more than 300 percent. Homesteaders, farmers, and small-scale ranchers transformed the open range by fencing off smaller and smaller parcels.

Cattle kingpins fought back. They hired out-of-state muscle to cut down fences and protect their herds from rustling, or so they claimed. Six cattlemen lynched two homesteaders in south central Wyoming in 1889. Two years later, a man named Nate Champion drew the hatred of big cattlemen throughout the region when he became an informal spokesman for small-time local ranchers.

The first attempt on Champion's life ended with one would-be assassin dead and two witnesses who were later murdered before they could testify. Champion planned to testify against his attackers, but five months later a group of fifty-two armed men stormed into the town of Buffalo in Johnson County to shut Champion up for good.

The posse of Wyoming ranchers and gunmen all the way from Texas cornered Champion at a ranch south of town, where he and a friend fought them off for an entire day. Champion kept a journal during the siege, its entries a record of increasing desperation:

Me and Nick Ray was getting breakfast when the attack took place.

Nick is shot but not dead yet.

Nick is dead. He died about 9 o'clock.

Boys, I feel pretty lonesome just now. I wish there was someone with me so we could watch all sides at once.

Well they have just got through shelling the house like hail. I hear them splitting wood. I guess they are going to fire the house tonight. I think I will make a break when night comes, if alive.

The house is all fired. Goodbye, boys, if I never see you again.

Champion sprinted out shooting as the cabin went up in flames. He was cut down in seconds. One of his murderers pinned a note to his corpse: "Cattle Thieves, Beware!"

Two days later hundreds of enraged locals retaliated against the hired guns who had hunted Champion. After a three-day standoff, army troops from nearby Fort McKinney arrived and took the invaders into custody, but the perpetrators were politically well connected, and the Johnson County War ended without any charges filed.

Still, the reign of the cattle barons was ending, the huge ranches steadily replaced by smaller ones or farm fields of buckwheat, potatoes, and corn. As the turn of the century drew near, Cheyenne slipped into depression. Stores closed and mansions stood empty. As one Union Pacific agent put it, "Times were hard and Cheyenne practically dead." The city needed an economic infusion of some kind, something that would simultaneously leverage the railroad, the local cowboy talent, and the energy that had made it, at least briefly, the cattle capital of the West.

Cheyenne needed a rodeo.

5

AN ATTRACTIVE AND
NOVEL PROGRAM

ONE DAY IN THE summer of 1897, Frederick Angier was sitting on a fence near the train tracks in Cheyenne, watching a group of cowboys try to coax a horse onto a rail car. The animal was having none of it, and the skirmish raised a cloud of dust and noise.

Angier was riveted, then inspired. As a traveling passenger agent for the Union Pacific Railroad, it was his job to look for ways to fill more seats. People would pay to see this kind of muscular drama, Angier thought. Small rodeos had begun cropping up around the region, showcasing the practical skills and athleticism that were still very much part of daily life in the West. But they were all local affairs. Host a big rodeo, a truly one-of-a-kind event, Angier reasoned, and people would not just pay to see it—they would *travel* to see it.

Just the year before, spectators had journeyed all the way to Athens, Greece, to watch athletes from fourteen countries compete in the first modern Olympic Games. Angier thought of the railway bringing visitors from both coasts, as well as from Denver and points south. There was even a decent marketing hook: 1897 marked the thirtieth anniversary of the first train into Cheyenne.

Rodeo came from the Spanish word for roundup, and in the days of New Spain it meant just that: seasonal gatherings for the purpose of branding calves, separating mixed herds, and getting animals ready for market. As ranching culture made its way to the United States, cowboys also embraced the vaqueros' tradition of friendly competition. In their downtime, cowboys held races and competed at tasks like cutting cows out of a herd, roping calves, and subduing stubborn horses.

The ends of cattle drives brought men from different outfits together in the nearest cow town. Drinking and visiting brothels were part of the equation, of course, but so were informal contests pitting men from rival ranches against one another. Whether to settle a bet, back up a boast, or just pass the time, sporting rivalry became part of the cowboy life.

The first impromptu contests happened in local corrals, with only ranch hands and maybe a few people from the surrounding area for an audience. As crowds started to grow, rodeos moved to larger stockyard corrals with more space for action and audiences.

A bronco busting contest held in Deer Trail, Colorado, on the Fourth of July in 1869 may have been the first organized rodeo in the United States. Men from the Campstool, Hashknife, and Mill Iron Ranches took turns seeing how long they could stay in the saddle. An Englishman named Emilnie Gardenshire took the honors on a horse named Montana Blizzard.

He earned the title of "Champion Bronco Buster of the Plains" and a new suit of clothes.

In 1872, a spectator event dubbed the "Old Glory Blowout" was held at a racetrack in North Platte, Nebraska, also on the Fourth of July. It included calf roping and buffalo riding, and coincided with Nebraska's last great open-range roundup. A decade later, a group of cowboys at a saloon in Pecos, Texas, decided to hold their own competition. Local ranchers put up $40 for the winners in steer roping and bronco busting. The Frontier Days Rodeo in Prescott, Arizona, on the Fourth of July 1888, was the first to invite competitors and charge an admission fee. The festivities included fireworks, bicycle races, and greased pig catching.

It's no coincidence that all these early events were held on the same date. At the time, the Fourth of July was one of the most important public holidays of the year. More than a celebration of the young country's birthday, it was a day for Americans in communities of all sizes, from New England to the western frontier, to feel like they were part of the entity called the United States. The recent trauma of the Civil War only made the holiday more meaningful, a way to reaffirm a sense of union. As Prescott's newspaper put it:

The patriotic demonstration of 112 years ago, when old Independence Bell sent forth its peal to herald the adoption of the Declaration of Independence, was scarcely less enthusiastic than was the demonstration yesterday of the citizens of this section, away out here on the so-called borderlines of civilization.

One of the first documented rodeo events in Wyoming, then still a territory, took place at a huge ranch near Casper owned by the Swan Land and Cattle Company. Also known as the Two-Bar, the ranch once managed holdings larger than the state of Connecticut. In the early 1880s, the Swan cowboys put on a show for Scottish and English landowners, some of whom had traveled from Europe to watch the men race horses, ride steers, and challenge Native Americans in tug-of-war. Local legend says that Butch Cassidy, still a law-abiding cowhand at the time, gave a demonstration of marksmanship with a pistol.

Angier ran his rodeo idea past the editor of the *Cheyenne Daily Sun-Leader*, who knew as well as anyone that Cheyenne needed something to fill the hole left by the cratering cattle market. Other cities had agricultural festivals—northern Colorado alone had a Pickle Day, a Potato Day, and a Corn Roast—and Denver's pioneer-themed Festival of Mountain and Plain was an enviable success. Even Lander, Wyoming, had staged a public horse race, and that town barely had five hundred people.

Cheyenne didn't have squat. As one local businessman put it: "We can't have a crop show. We don't raise anything in Cheyenne except hell."

But the once Holy City of the Cow did have advantages: top cowpunchers, a rough-and-tumble reputation, and the railway. Cheyenne had already hosted an exhibition of Texas-style steer riding on the Fourth of July 1872, and the following year a bronco-riding contest kicked up dust on Sixteenth Street. "There was quite a crowd and some quiet swearing," reported the *Daily Leader*, while also noting that the middle of downtown might not be the best place for future roughriding events:

"Suppose one of these broncos should run up the side of a brick building to the roof, or up a telegraph pole to the cross-bars and insulators, would the rider keep his seat? These broncos are liable to do these things: we have known them to do worse."

There was legitimate concern that bronco riding was too violent for widespread appeal. In May 1897, a "Wild West exhibition" at the Cheyenne territorial fairgrounds had to be halted after a number of competitors were hurt. (The crowd was small, the papers noted, "owing to a general dislike of such sport.") The following weekend a group of Wyoming cowboys put on another amateur show in town that ended in tragedy. One rider was bucked so hard he did a full somersault in midair and landed on his back. He hurt his hip and spine so badly that he eventually died.

But prominent Cheyenne businessmen liked Angier's rodeo idea and put out a call for donations to hold a major summertime event. They raised $562, including one contribution of 25 cents. A newspaper editorial in late August announced that Cheyenne Frontier Days would be held September 23—less than one month away.

It was a scramble to get ready. The first order of business was cleaning up the place. Newspaper announcements urged residents and businesses to put all their trash cans and empty boxes and barrels out of sight. The city marshal set chain gangs to work clearing away trash from streets and alleys and hauling it to the dump.

Posters hung throughout Wyoming and Colorado advertised "An Attractive and Novel Program" that would include "Vivid Representation of Frontier Scenes: Pony Express,

Emigrant Schooners, Vigilantes, Wild Broncho Riding, Roping, Throwing and other Cowboy Feats, Pony Races, Pioneer Sports, Etc." An eight-page souvenir pamphlet listed twelve events alongside ads for hotels, grocers, shoe stores, and ladies' wool underwear.

From its inception, Frontier Days deliberately tapped into the sentiment that something special was disappearing. In 1890, the year Wyoming became the forty-fourth state, the U.S. Census announced the end of the frontier, at least officially. It was a turning point in American history: the distinction between settled and unsettled territory was gone. As the program for the first Frontier Days put it:

> The frontier line of advancing settlements has already disappeared, like misty shadows vanishing before the Sun's Rays. The varied and adventurous life of the early explorers, the hunters and trappers and Indian fighters, the dangers and privations of the first settlers and the thrilling incidents of their struggles on mountains and plain, are now dissolving views of memory, like the "passing of ships in the night."

The Old West would soon be gone, but the romanticizing was just beginning.

IN THE DAYS LEADING up to the contest, men from Wyoming, Colorado, and Nebraska began to arrive in Cheyenne by horseback and wagon team. Trains brought visitors by the hundreds; Angier had arranged to have round-trip tickets from Denver offered at a discount. Spectators arrived to find a freshly scrubbed city that was ready for action. American flags and red, white, and blue bunting hung from buildings and balconies.

The first battalion of the U.S. Army's 8th Infantry Regiment marched from Fort Russell and set up camp near the fairgrounds. When they were done pitching their light A-frame tents, the men were dismissed for some rest and recuperation. The night before the big day, the city's saloons, restaurants, hotels, and streets overflowed with people. Impeccably dressed aldermen from Denver mingled with cowhands still dusty from the trail; army lieutenants tipped their hats to ladies from Laramie; tourists from the Midwest gawked at bowlegged cowboys dressed in silk shirts and sheepskin chaps. Brass bands and the U.S. Army provided the soundtrack. Anyone who couldn't find a hotel room could hire a berth in railroad sleeping cars hauled in for the occasion.

The next morning visitors and nearly all of Cheyenne's residents headed for the fairgrounds—on foot and horseback, in wagons and carriages, and aboard special Union Pacific trains running hourly from the downtown depot. A dozen emigrant wagons that happened to be passing through Wyoming on the Oregon Trail joined the procession. Drawn by teams of oxen, the prairie schooners trailed horses, dogs, and children.

At noon, a special excursion train from Denver pulled into the Cheyenne depot and was greeted by a head-ringing cacophony. As the clock struck the hour, every church and school bell in the city rang, and every railroad engine and business blew its whistle. Fort Russell's Battery A lit off thirty cannons, and hundreds of locals fired pistols, rifles, and shotguns into the sky. Cheyenne Frontier Days was officially under way.

The fairground corrals teemed with nervous livestock and men doing their best to keep the animals under control. Stray dogs nipped the heels of lowing cattle. Admission to the grounds was free, but a spot in the uncovered bleachers cost 15 cents. For 20 cents more, spectators could find a seat in the grandstand, where high-society men and women in summer fashions enjoyed "temperate and spirituous libations." On either side of the seating area, crowds packed against the fence surrounding the half-mile track. Some sat astride horses or in carriages.

The first three events were horse races. Prizes ranged from $20 to $50, the equivalent of roughly $500 to $1,400 today. The wild horse race delivered authentic frontier-style fun. Ownerless horses were part of life in the West, where tens of thousands of mustangs still ran free. Earlier in the day, cowboys had gathered about fifty wild horses in the corral at the fairground. These were fierce, agile animals that had never been roped, much less saddled or ridden. Now ten of them were lassoed and led to the track in front of the grandstand. Twenty men stood ready, a rider and an assistant for each.

When the contest official shouted, "Go!" two men sprang at each horse and tried to strap a bridle and saddle on the terrified animal. This was the start of fifteen minutes of absolute madness. Horses bucked, kicked, bolted, screamed, or simply lay down.

Overeager spectators kept crowding onto the track, despite repeated warnings. One *Wyoming State Tribune* reporter judged this as excessively risky for women: "It is a curious and inexplicable thing, the unaccountable desire of dozens of ladies to stand on the racetrack, totally oblivious to the extreme novelty and danger of their position." To his relief, they eventually hiked up their petticoats and removed themselves to a safe distance. A number of "sturdy citizens" were called into service to help police keep the crowd back.

By the time the winner of the wild horse race managed to ride his mount all the way around the half-mile track, some of the mustangs hadn't even been saddled yet. The event was over, but the wild horses weren't finished. Later in the afternoon, they broke out of their corral and stampeded up the racetrack. The herd turned and drove straight at—and then through—the bleachers, splintering planks and parting the crowd like a screaming sea. God knows how, but no one was badly injured.

Anyone who thought the wild horse race would be the day's most exciting event had to reconsider when the bucking horses were led into the arena. The struggling animals could barely be contained inside the track, and kept knocking over men trying to put on bridles and saddles. Sometimes a cowboy would bite or twist a horse's ear to distract it when the saddle was being slid into place. In the words of one witness, "The scene of the wildest kind of beasts raving and jumping and attempting to jump the fences kept the crowd at a distance and presented a thrilling scene."

Bronco busting—teaching a horse to accept a saddle and rider—was a legitimate job in cattle country. Riders earned good money for each horse they broke. But there weren't any standards or rules at the time for judging bronco riding as sport.

Each man just had to hold on as long as he could and hope the horse put on a good show for the judges. Unlike today's eight-second time limit, the ride went on until the horse stopped bucking, the rider was thrown off, or the judges decided they had seen enough. There were a few rules for the cowboys: they could use only a plain halter and a single braided rein held in one hand. If the rider's other hand touched any part of the rigging, known as "pulling leather," it meant disqualification. Beyond that, a cowboy just had to not get killed.

When each man was ready, he yelled, "Jerk 'er!" An assistant yanked the blindfold off the horse and got out of the way as the snorting bronco went ballistic. Each animal bucked differently. Horses reared on their hind legs and switched directions in midair. One second an animal would crowhop—make stiff-legged jumps—or "swallow its head" by arching its back. The next moment it would sunfish, twisting its body into a crescent as if trying to touch nose to tail. Other movements were dubbed the double O, the corkscrew, and the high dive.

Riders had a choice of techniques to both infuriate the horse and stay aboard for an extra fraction of a second. A cowboy might kick the animal in the ribs or fan it with his hat to get its blood up. For further encouragement he could jam a thumb in a sensitive spot in the horse's shoulder to make it buck harder. Sometimes fans even chanted, "Thumb him! Thumb him!" Other cowboys found that a little gum resin on the chaps helped keep them stuck to the saddle.

The bronco riding at the first Frontier Days "was pronounced by old timers as equal to anything they ever witnessed," declared the *Daily Leader*. Bill Jones of La Grande,

Wyoming, was the winner, becoming the first in a long line of local champions.

On the frontier, most people believed that bucking couldn't be trained or forced; certain horses had it in their blood. Owners pampered their prizewinners like star athletes. Yet some saw bronco busting as animal cruelty. That year, the Colorado Humane Society sent a representative to monitor the action. When the man started to lecture a small group of onlookers about how the show should be canceled, "two cowboys gently slipped a rope over him and took him to the buffalo corral, where they tied him up with the buffalo for the afternoon, releasing him just in time to take the excursion train back to Denver."

Between contests, the Frontier Days audience enjoyed skits and dramatizations of recent events that were fast becoming part of western lore. At one point, six draft horses pulled an old Deadwood stagecoach onto the track. Masked men playing the part of highwaymen gave chase, firing blanks into the air, but before they could complete the holdup, a rescue party of armed cowboys saved the day. It was a scene many residents of the Wyoming Territory could relate to or may have even lived through.

In a nod to Cheyenne's lawless early years, a mock vigilante committee, "masked and armed to the teeth," pulled a Laramie humorist and newspaperman from the grandstand and hustled him toward a makeshift gallows across the track. He played along until the noose was dangling over his head. Then he finally said, "This is carrying a joke too far, boys," and ducked away under the judging stand. The vigilantes strung up a dummy in his place and riddled it with bullets in front of the crowd.

When it grew too dark to hold the steer-roping contest as planned, the first ever Frontier Days was over. The whole event took only about six hours. But for the four thousand people who were there, the celebration had delivered on its promise of spectacle, sport, and thrill. A visitor from Toledo, Ohio, said: "I am a surgeon in a State Insane Asylum, and used to excitement, but Cheyenne takes the cake." That evening, the winners collected their prizes and day-trippers boarded trains back to Denver. The 1st Cavalry Regiment band played at the depot as the cars rolled out, trailing cheers from open windows. Everyone else filled the streets with carousing, dancing, and innocent gunfire.

After running the numbers, Frontier Days organizers concluded that the first large-scale rodeo in history had nearly broken even. Public opinion was more conclusive. As one newspaper pronounced, Cheyenne had just hosted "the greatest and most successful occasion ever celebrated in the West."

PART II

6

WARRIORS TO WRANGLERS

KUA PURDY WAS BORN on Christmas Eve 1873 at Mānā, the Parker family residence just outside Waimea. At that time of year, imported trees and bushes like holly, magnolia, and hydrangea bloomed around the estate, which was fast becoming a social and economic hub of the island. The Parkers would have been hosting Christmas services and parties, balancing Bible verse and libation in equal portions, as well as festivities highlighted by hula dancing and ukulele.

Across the cobbled road of the main compound, cattle grazed in pastures surrounding the small family cemetery where patriarch John Palmer Parker was buried. In a clearing a few miles west, toward Waimea, pansies planted by Jack Purdy bloomed around the stone house he built in the 1830s.*

In Hawaiian terms, baby Ikua had the *koko*, the blood, of royalty. On his mother's side, he was the great-great-great-grandson of Kamehameha I, the towering warrior who had

---

*Because of Purdy, the pansy became a symbol of paniolo culture, worn to this day by riders during festivals and parades.

unified the Hawaiian Islands. Harry Purdy, Ikua's father, came from a line of esteemed cattlemen and was himself an accomplished Parker Ranch cowboy. Ikua's uncles John, George, and James were all renowned paniolo. But the ancestor whose life perhaps most influenced Ikua's destiny was his grandfather, the legendary bullock hunter Jack Purdy.

ONE EVENING IN THE fall of 1857, two Frenchmen who were touring the island of Hawaii sat down in a saloon in Waimea. They were captivated by the spell of Mauna Kea and wanted to hire a guide to lead them to the summit. When the Frenchmen asked around, the response was almost unanimous: they needed to talk to "the best rider in the Islands, the most fearless hunter of wild bullocks, the man who knows best the forest trails and the mountain passes . . . in sheer daring no one surpasses Jack Purdy."

Stalking and killing Hawaii's wild cattle had become a notoriously dangerous profession, one that "put tiger hunting to blush and made capturing wild elephants seem a small thing." Visitors and explorers traded tales of the hunters' wild adventures and regular brushes with death on the slopes of the volcano.

Purdy, age fifty-seven, was known for his backcountry resourcefulness and a stamina that bordered on superhuman. He agreed to meet the two men, and as the evening progressed, Purdy downed "slug after slug of small glasses of gin, which seemed to have no effect other than to give him courage to lay aside his normal taciturnity." They settled on a price—250 francs, plus tip—and agreed to rendezvous at daybreak the next morning. Then Purdy proceeded to tell a story that would help cement his legacy in Hawaiian lore.

There was an Englishman in the islands named Julius Brenchley, Purdy said, a capable and undaunted beast of a man. Brenchley had once walked from St. Louis to British Columbia, where he then sailed for Hawaii. Like so many travelers before him, he fell in love with the place and stayed.

Brenchley was a seasoned mountain man and horseback rider, and it wasn't long before he and Purdy met. The two became friends, of a sort. Like the small handful of other men who had the right stuff to make a living in the hills, they developed a gentlemanly rivalry marked by "comradely taunts and monosyllabic aggressions from behind a mask of polite manners and chivalrous restraint." The result was an ongoing "contest in audacity, in which neither the one nor the other came out the final victor."

That is, until the incident with the bullock. Purdy and Brenchley were on a multiday trek toward Mauna Loa, the island's second highest summit, packing nothing except rifles and blankets. They slept at the snowline the first night and continued uphill the next morning. Along the way they shot and ate ducks, goose, and other wild birds. But soon they ran out of gunpowder—an oversight so obvious it suggests they had also packed ample booze—and in short order were out of food.

If they pushed hard, Purdy said, he knew a place "where wild bulls abounded." They hiked another twenty miles before coming upon an area of marshy swamp.

Brenchley, standing ankle-deep in muck, was skeptical. "Where are your wild bulls?" he asked.

"There, in the woods," Purdy said coolly.

"And how shall we attack them?"

"There are any number of ways," Purdy said. "I shall turn the bull over to you when he can no longer defend himself— the rest will be your problem."

With that, Purdy took off into the trees. A few minutes later Brenchley heard the familiar sound of snapping branches and trampling hooves. It was a full-grown bull, charging straight for him.

The animal was fifty yards away and closing fast. But when it tried to cross a pool of mud, the bull's feet sank deep. In seconds it was trapped, unable to do anything except to toss its head and roar in frustration.

Purdy emerged from the thicket, muddy and self-satisfied. "So there's our dinner," he said. "All we need to do is kill the creature."

Brenchley asked how on earth they could do that without being trapped or gored.

"Why, I thought you had the courage and dash for that," Purdy said, starting to gather marsh rushes. He tied them into two bundles and used them to make his way across the mud, alternately standing on one and moving the other forward. When he reached the entrapped animal, he took out his hunting knife and killed it with a single thrust.

Brenchley stood speechless as his rival cut a large slab from the bull's side and leapfrogged his way back across the mud. Before long they had a fire going, the giant bloody steak sizzling on hot rocks around the edge.

Did Purdy embellish? Perhaps. Yet his account is a window

onto the very real challenges that Hawaii's bullock hunters and wranglers faced. This environment was light-years from the beachy, palm-shaded Hawaii of popular imagination, and working cattle here was as difficult and deadly as it was anywhere.

ONE OF THE FIRST outsiders to document the work of the paniolo was the British explorer and travel writer Isabella Lucy Bird. Bird took her first overseas adventure to the United States in 1854 at age twenty-three, on doctors' orders to help cure depression and insomnia. The book that trip inspired, *The Englishwoman in America*, was the first of a series of bestsellers that lyrically chronicled extensive tours across the Middle East, Africa, Asia, and, as they were still known at the time, the Sandwich Islands.

Bird's writing and photography of faraway places was vivid and unvarnished. "This side of Hawaii to my thinking is hideous," she later wrote of her 1873 visit to the island's rocky and arid northwest.

She was more appreciative of the climb from the coast to the highlands:

> Every hundred feet of ascent from the rainless, fervid beach of Kawaihae increased the freshness of the temperature, and rendered exercise more delightful. From the fringe of palms along the coast to the damp hills north of Waimea . . . there is not a tree or stream, though the scorched earth is deeply scored by the rush of fierce temporary torrents . . . No water, no grass, no

ferns . . . The red soil becomes suffused with a green
tinge ten miles from the beach, and at the summit of
the ascent the desert blends with this beautiful Waimea
plain, one of the most marked features of Hawaii . . .
There were frame houses sheltered from the winds by
artificial screens of mulberry trees, and from the in-
cursions of cattle by rough walls of lava stones five feet
high . . .

On Hawaii, Bird found a multiethnic mix that would become even more diverse with the arrival of immigrants and
laborers from the Americas, Europe, and Asia. Hawaii owed its
remarkable diversity in part to its location; it was the perfect
place to break up a long sea voyage and resupply. A taste of life
in the islands was enough to convince many visitors to stay and
build new lives. Imported labor for Hawaii's industries, particularly sugar, added to the diverse milieu.

And with each culture came new traditions. Portuguese immigrants brought the machête de braça, a small four-stringed
instrument that, when it was retuned and its metal strings replaced with gut, became the ukulele. Newcomers from China
and Japan introduced new foods and farming techniques, and
opened businesses that became cornerstones of commerce in
towns like Lahaina, Hilo, and Waimea.*

---

* In 1878, the Chinese revolutionary Sun Yat-sen moved to Maui at age thirteen to live with his brother, a successful businessman. He attended the 'Iolani School in Honolulu, then returned to China to lead the 1911 revolution
and become the first president of the Republic of China.

Yet racial mixing only went so far. Laborers on sugar plantations lived in separate camps based on ethnicity. On ranches, the first Japanese immigrants were assigned menial work like building fences and nicknamed *opae*, Hawaiian for shrimp. (Later generations of Japanese in Hawaii became respected cowboys.) The ranch owners were *haole*, white (Caucasian), as were most of the ranch managers, or *luna*. There was even a song that satirized the arrogant *haole luna* astride his white horse, coming to kick the other cowboys.

Still, life in nineteenth-century Hawaii was hard enough that it forced people to cooperate. In ranching communities, the demands of the work fostered integration with and acceptance of people of different backgrounds. At remote cabins and workstations across Mauna Kea and other up-country areas, paniolo lived under the same roofs as fence crews, cooks, and other workers. A soak in a Japanese-style *furo*, or wood-heated bath, was the reward for a long day on the mountain. Everyone ate from the same plates of pork, chicken, fish, and pickled vegetables, using chopsticks whittled on the spot from tree branches.

In the evenings, cowboys and other ranch hands would drink gin or cognac by the light of kerosene lamps. Beneath a nighttime sky almost bright enough to read by, they sat around sharpening tools, braiding lariats, or telling stories. Someone always had a ukulele, and after a few drinks, nobody noticed the smell of fresh animal hides laid out around the camp to dry.

Waking at two or three A.M. to a breakfast of pancakes, coffee, and the occasional swig of gin, the paniolo would set out for the day. Each man often brought a second horse along to ride when the first mount got too tired. The most common trail grub was strips of fresh beef the paniolo tied to their saddles to dry into jerky in the sun, another trick learned from the vaqueros. They also carried dried mountain oysters—bull testicles, rich in iron—or pounded taro that they would shave into small pieces and eat together with salted beef.

Paniolo often preferred to work under the stars, when the wild cattle came out of the forests to visit watering spots. Riding quietly along a trail, the cowboys would light matches to look for tracks on the ground. They followed the animals along foggy hillsides or into ravines, making sure to stay downwind. Ears tuned for a rustle of branches or cracking sticks, they waited for the ideal moment to give chase.

Spoken Hawaiian was the language of the range and the towns that bordered it. Paniolo communicated in their native tongue, often in single-word barks that got the point across instantly in a potentially dangerous situation: *lio* for horse, *pā'eke* for corral, *pipi* for cow (from the English word *beef*). Paniolo had to be *maka'ala* (careful) when riding around *nā pohā* (sinkholes), and sometimes had to *'oki hao* (dehorn) an animal before using the *hao kuni* (branding iron).*

Living in remote ranch stations meant paniolo were separated from their families and the comforts of town life for

---

*During the twentieth century, the world of the paniolo became a critical reservoir for preserving the language, as it came under assault by missionary and government policies intended to eradicate Hawaiian altogether.

weeks at a time. Cowboys sometimes rode downhill on Sundays to visit, covering up to 25 miles and 7,500 vertical feet. Along the way they might try to bag a *pua'a* (pig) or two for a special dinner. In the early hours of the next morning, they would ride all the way back up to camp.

It wasn't always family members paniolo stopped in to visit. Hilo, the port town on the eastern side of Hawaii, was close to the major sugar plantations and the center of the business boom that followed in the 1860s. ("Except sugar and dollars," wrote Isabella Bird, "one rarely hears any subject spoken about with general interest.") Some women in Hilo took cowboys in almost like strays. These *wahine manuahi* were not prostitutes, nor were they looked down upon for these extramarital relationships. The Hawaiian term roughly translates as "free-giving woman," carrying the idea of a mistress but without the moral judgment.

BIRD, AN EXPERIENCED RIDER who covered thousands of miles on horseback during her own travels, could see the paniolo were outstanding riders, as were Hawaiian women. Visiting Oahu in January 1873, she noted that "women seemed perfectly at home in their gay, brass-bossed high peaked saddles, flying along astride, barefooted, with their orange and scarlet riding dresses streaming on each side beyond their horses' tails, a bright kaleidoscopic flash of bright eyes, white teeth, shining hair, garlands of flowers and many coloured dresses." In one of Bird's illustrations, titled "The Pa-u or Hawaiian Ladies' Holiday

Riding Dress," the rider looks calm while the horse, all four legs off the ground, is clearly running at a gallop.[*]

Foreigners like Bird also took note of the paniolo's skill with the lasso. A Hawaiian cowboy's life depended on his *kaula 'ili*, or lariat. They made their own ropes from a single cowhide, cut into strips and braided together. (Rawhide lasted longer in the humid climate than the manila-fiber ropes used on the mainland.) Paniolo gave their ropes Hawaiian names, for luck, attitude, or both, and as a sign that they treated them with care.

The paniolo's other gear was well adapted to the environment. Wide-brimmed lightweight hats woven from pandanus leaves shielded their heads from the rain and their eyes from the unforgiving tropical sun. In the cold fog and wet forests at higher elevation, they wore long ponchos that they rolled up and tied to the saddles when the work brought them down the mountain and into the heat. Over tall lace-up boots they strapped leather chaps for protection from thorny underbrush or the occasional horse or bullock hoof. Thick leather stirrup coverings, called *tapaderos*, protected their feet from rocks and sharp branches, and added extra heft when a cowboy had to kick an uncooperative animal.

The process of bringing in a wild bullock started with roping an animal that weighs three-quarters of a ton, from up to fifty feet away. The paniolo in pursuit aimed his lasso at the

---

[*]Lucy Thurston, an American missionary who arrived in Kailua-Kona in the 1820s, rode sidesaddle when she first arrived in the islands. Many years later, a witness to Ms. Thurston's riding noted that she "rides astride & wears spurs."

head, sometimes while riding at top speed. A miss could still be effective if the loop ended up around a limb and tripped the animal. But success with the lasso did not mark the end of the duel. As Yale man Francis Allyn Olmsted observed in 1840: "And now, be wary for thy life bold hunter; for the savage animal is maddened with terror . . . eye-balls glaring with fire and his frame quivering with rage." Having a well-trained horse was never more essential than when the tormented bullock turned on its pursuer. The rider had to work with his mount to dodge the bullock's charges and simultaneously bring the animal to the ground. Sometimes the cowboy had to yank the enraged animal off its feet over and over until it became relatively docile.

If the hide was to be harvested on the spot, the paniolo was off his mount in a flash, brandishing a skinning knife. Stepping around the animal's head and horns, he hamstrung the bullock with two swift cuts to the hind legs. Then he was back onto his horse to capture more animals. Only at the end of the day did he return to kill the injured bullocks, skin them, and drape the hides over his saddle for the ride back to the ranch cabin.

More often, though, the paniolo wanted to round up bullocks, and for this they had to lead the lassoed animals to captivity while staying a safe distance from those wicked horns. If the animal refused to submit, the next step was to tie the other end of the lasso to a tree and leave the bullock to thrash itself into exhaustion, sometimes overnight. When the cowboy returned, the animals would be more cooperative and more easily led into captivity. (Another common technique for controlling rogue animals was to tether the captured bullock to a *pini*, a tame cow or bull that would calm the wild one and help lead it down the mountain.)

As a precaution, paniolo sometimes sawed a bullock's horns off; but even a weakened, hornless bullock could still be dangerous. While his horse led the cow or bull through sun-dappled forests and across gritty plains and lava fields, the rider had to stay alert, ready for anything. (An old vaquero saying also applied to paniolo: a man with a lassoed bullock rode "tied to death.") If the bullock gathered enough energy to charge again, the paniolo had to gallop a safe distance away while still connected by the rawhide rope. A paniolo would do anything to avoid the shame of cutting an animal free and losing his lasso, even if it might mean injury or worse. Like sailors reading subtle cues in the wind and waves, paniolo had to be acutely aware of changes in rope tension and adjust accordingly. Pulling too hard on a lassoed animal could snap a lariat; a loop of slack line could trip a horse, throwing or crushing its rider.

When enough cattle were corralled, paniolo led them down to Waimea in ground-shaking drives that, in the words of one 1859 newspaper account, could be spied first as "a great cloud of dust some three or four miles up the mountain side." When leading animals, cowboy and horse still had to contend with precarious trails and loose, jagged lava rocks that snapped horses' ankles and sent riders flying. Camouflaged bullock pits from days past occasionally swallowed up men and mounts, as did hidden holes of collapsed lava tubes, concealed under a mat of greenery. Head injuries from kicks or falls were common and often fatal.

An early Parker Ranch cowboy described what to do when
a horse and rider went down:

> If man and horse are moving, there's a chance they will
> come up smiling. If not, they are dead. If the horse is bad
> hurt you drive your legging-knife into the spinal cord
> just back of his head. He kicks a couple of times, but he
> is out of misery. If the man is just hurt, you take him up
> behind you on your horse, back to the station for help.
> If he is dead you take him over your horse, your heart
> sick inside. At the station you lay him out and cover
> him with his yellow saddle-slicker until someone can
> take him home to be buried. The drive goes on. The
> work has to be done.

Even the vegetation posed a threat: the inch-long thorns of
the *kiawe* (mesquite) tree could blind a horse or leave an un-
lucky rider with a puncture wound that invited gangrene. And,
as in the American West, Hawaiian cowboys always needed to
keep the next water source in mind. Many parts of the archipelago are stunningly verdant; the Iao Valley on Maui receives
almost 400 inches of rain a year, making it one of the wettest
places in the world. But in other areas, especially along Hawaii's
west coast, freshwater sources are scarce. Without careful plan-
ning, a long cattle drive in the midday sun could turn into a
catastrophe.

Bullock hunting and working cattle were both dangerous, but at least hunters could shoot an animal as a last resort.

Paniolo had to deliver cattle alive, first to the ranches and then to corrals at Kawaihae and other ports on Hawaii's west coast. The route was downhill, and by now the animals were mostly under control. Still, the journey had many of the same hazards as the upland transfer: thorny brush, little water, sharp rocks underfoot, and blazing temperatures.

Once they made it to the coast, there remained one more step in the wrangling process, the one that truly put the paniolo in their own category: herding into the surf.

Because harbors like Kawaihae were too shallow for large ships, the steamships that ferried the cattle to the slaughter-house in Honolulu or to markets overseas had to anchor out past the reef. So the island's cattle, after surviving the arduous drive from the highlands to the shore, now had to swim.* One at a time, paniolo roped bullocks around the neck and led them down to the beach. Eyeing the waves like surfers, the riders carefully counted the breakers until the right moment came to plunge forward, cow in tow. Dogs sometimes helped by nipping at the animals' heels.

Thinking they were being given one last chance to catch a cowboy, bullocks would usually charge straight toward the waves after the horse and rider. If they refused to step into the sea, a second cowboy had to grab the animal's tail and pull it sideways until the waves started to knock it over, which usually convinced it to swim.

Past the breakers, the cowboy had to steer his horse—now

---

* Kailua-Kona was another major cattle-shipping port, as was Napoʻopoʻo at Kealakekua Bay.

shoulder-deep or, more often, swimming—toward a whaleboat approaching the shore. He threw the rope to one of the crewmen, who pulled the animal in, put a halter around its neck, and tied it to the gunwale before tossing the paniolo his rope back. Soaked in sweat and salt water, the cowboys turned to shore to do it all over again.

For this work, paniolo used specially trained "shipping horses" that were larger and more confident swimmers, and rode saddles that were mostly made of wood, which lasted longer in salt water. Still, no amount of specialized equipment or training guaranteed successful or even safe operations at the shore. Bad timing with a wave or a moment of fumbling by the whaleboat crew could end with a horse upended in the surf, putting both animal and rider in peril.

And then there were the sharks. The reefs that protected the harbors used for loading cattle were favorite feeding grounds for marine predators. On loading days, sharks sometimes congregated near the whaleboats, nosing for steak tartare. Sailors used rifles to scare them away, even dynamite on occasion.

One May morning in 1884, Sam Parker, John Palmer Parker's grandson, was helping load cattle onto a steamship at Kawaihae. The work was going well when, in a blur of teeth and blood, a massive shark suddenly bit a swimming calf in two. This could not stand, and the men in the whaleboat gave chase. They managed to stick a harpoon in the shark, but even then it dragged the boat through the waves like a child's toy, a Hawaiian version of the "Nantucket sleigh ride" that New England whalers described after harpooning a humpback. Finally, the exhausted shark relented. Parker and the cowboys used their lassos to haul the monster to shore and onto the beach. A quick measurement showed it was eighteen feet long and almost six feet around. Parker cut off the head to keep as a souvenir.

To load the big ships, paniolo brought animals out to the whaleboat one at a time until it had six or eight attached. The crew then rowed to the steamship, flanked by swimming cattle. To lift them onto the ship, paniolo had to fit each bullock into a crude lifting harness. The process required at least one man to be in the water with the animals, clinging to each one's back to affix a sling under its belly. ("Anyone who has seen Hawaii cattle knows that there is a good deal of excitement connected with getting on their backs, whether they are in the water or not," read the *Hawaiian Star*.)

Eventually, each cow was lifted straight out of the water, soaked and bellowing, and deposited on the deck of the ship. In extreme cases when a bullock couldn't be harnessed, mariners in the longboats tied ropes around the animal's horns and neck and pulled it onto the steamship's deck.

Inevitably, cattle were sometimes hurt or drowned. Others would get loose and swim for freedom. On one occasion, a bullock escaped its harness and plunged into the ocean. A witness recalled how a cowboy "stripped down to his britches and started off after that steer." In rough seas a mile from shore, he swam to the animal, "dived under it to get the sling rope untangled from his forelegs. Then he climbed onto the steer's back, lay down along its spine, took the horns in his hands and steered that animal ashore by hand pressure on the horns." The cowboy was Ikua Purdy's uncle, James.

―――――

HAZARDS ASIDE, THE LIFE of a paniolo also offered unequaled freedom and adventure. For a man who thrived on the satisfaction
of doing a difficult job well, on his own terms, there was no
better work than running cattle. This was as true in Hawaii as
it would soon be in the Wild West of North America.

Even the moments of greatest danger were balanced by a
sublimity that could inspire a cowboy to a kind of poetry. One
paniolo described the hyperalert, almost enchanted moment of
the hunt when the "mind is calm, ready":

> You hear the whispered command. You mount up and
> ride down over the rim. Down, down through the
> swirling fog and clutching brush. No need for silence
> now. Just watch which way those wily cattle are going
> to turn. Away from you, or right at you, head and horns
> set for the charge. Your pony steps aside, your hand
> flips a loop over the horns, you take up slack and your
> pony is turning, watching that rope, and you're run-
> ning beside the captive, then ahead of it, that beautiful
> Wild One.

These are the words of Eben Low, one of Hawaii's most
famous paniolo, a man who would almost single-handedly in-
troduce island cowboys and ranching to the wider world.

A great-grandson of John Palmer Parker, Eben was born in
1864 and grew up at the Parker Ranch. As a child, he made little

or no distinction between the ranch property and the expanse of Mauna Kea. The mountain was his playground, and Eben and his cousins explored and hunted wild pigs, goats, and sheep. Eben knew his way around horses and cattle before he became a teenager, and by the time he was twenty-six, he was already running a team of paniolo.

His gigantic middle name, Kahekawaipunaokauaamaluihi, meaning the flowing springwater from the rains at Maluihi, suited the man perfectly. He was loud, gregarious, and known for impulsivity, believing he came from "a pirate strain." His nickname, Rawhide Ben, may very well have been his own invention. He was not a drinker, but once, for no discernible reason, he shot the lights out in a local guesthouse, leaving patrons stunned.

But Eben was an indisputably gifted rider and roper. A visitor to Waimea once wrote that he could "find and ride through more rough country than any man I ever saw." To Eben, heaven was a ranch in Hawaii, surrounded by the beauty and bounty of the islands. "The paniolo work in the open," he once wrote, "in God's good sunlight and in His refreshing rains and winds."

He was also frequently in awe of the men he worked with— none more so than the Purdy family cowboys. One of Eben's favorite stories was about James Purdy, Ikua's uncle and the third son of Jack the bullock hunter, who had joined Eben and another paniolo on an excursion. They rode into a forest of koa and mamane, a place Eben described as "full of broken trees hidden by ferns and concealed lava tubes." It was a hell of a place to ride a horse, and "only fools and daredevils would attempt to ride fast, especially after wild cattle!" At one point the riders came upon about twenty bullocks a short distance up a narrow path. Eben dismounted and began sneaking toward the cattle through the curtain of vegetation. He held his .30-30 Winchester carbine ready, knowing that when the animals were startled, they would beeline for the obvious escape route: back along the same trail where he now stood.

The situation went from tense to critical in a flash. A bullock caught the cowboys' scent and panicked, setting off a stampede. Eben leapt sideways into the brush to avoid being flattened.

As soon as they passed, Eben stood and fired into the sky to warn the others. He followed the cattle and emerged from the forest certain he was too late and that he would soon come upon James's trampled corpse. But a moment later he heard a "voice of triumph" and rode quickly to the source. It was James Purdy, shirt torn and hat gone, standing over a huge bullock tied up at his feet.

They killed the animal, cut it into quarters, and hung them from the limb of a koa tree, out of reach of wild hogs. Later, they packed the hide and kidney fat home. In his journal, Eben gushed about James Purdy: "My joy for this man and his marvelous work and marvelous ride was beyond understanding."

While many paniolo fit the cowboy stereotype of taciturn men of action, Eben was an extrovert who seemed to have a limitless capacity for grandstanding. He even made sure to look the part, with his horseshoe mustache and, in some photos, a holstered six-shooter, a weapon paniolo had little use for.

Eben loved his job, but he also saw the impact ranching and wild cattle were having on his beloved island, and he worried about the long-term environmental consequences more

than most of his contemporaries. He had good reason to: by
1900, fully one-third of the land area of the Hawaiian archipelago was allocated for rangeland. "Forests everywhere have de-
creased and some seem to be drying up," Eben wrote. "This
is a sad sight." Cattle browsed new vegetation before it could
grow, and their hooves tore up the ground, hastening erosion.
One turn-of-the-century scientist noted: "I doubt that anything
in nature, axe and fire included, would have in the same space
of time brought the once densely clothed Islands to the present
condition . . . The changes have been brought to the benefit of
the very few, to the detriment of the whole Islands and community."

Yet in Eben's view, it was greed and the "desire for 'civilized' ways" that were to blame for Hawaii's ravaged beauty, not
ranching itself. His thinking revealed the unique relationship
Hawaiians had with cattle. They may be an invasive species in
the textbook sense, but they also had a kind of exalted status,
tracing back to their origins as the king's cattle. They had survived to become the foundation of an industry and proud
Hawaiian subculture that Eben Low, like Jack Purdy before him,
represented with verve.

Meanwhile, a world away in North America, another larger-
than-life character, an impresario in the saddle, was turning
cowboy culture into mainstream entertainment. In so doing,
he would embed the sport of rodeo and the cowboy spirit in the
soul of America.

7

SHOWTIME

I F THERE WAS A single living person who embodied the idea of the American West, it was William Frederick Cody. He was born in February 1846 near the hamlet of Le Claire in the Iowa Territory, just west of the Mississippi River. His parents, Isaac and Mary, came from pioneer families. Continuing this tradition, the Codys uprooted from Le Claire in 1853 and moved to a dirt-floor cabin in Kansas. There Isaac scraped together a living supplying lumber and other goods to nearby Fort Leavenworth and local tribes. As Cody put it later, "I spent all my spare time picking up the Kickapoo tongue from the Indian children in the neighborhood, and listening with both ears to the tales of the wide plains beyond." Willie's life was full of contradictions: one minute his father would be conducting peaceful business with the Kickapoo; the next saw him happily negotiating with troops who were the tip of the spear in the U.S. Army's campaign against native tribes.

If that wasn't confusing enough, his family was torn apart by the issue of slavery. His father was a staunch abolitionist, while his father's brother owned slaves. When Willie was ten, his father was stabbed after giving an antislavery speech, and died of his injuries.

Instead of being consumed by tragedy, Cody turned to a life of adventure. By the age of fifteen, he had already worked on a wagon train to Wyoming, had prospected for gold in Colorado, and was alleged to have ridden for the Pony Express. After serving as a scout for the 7th Volunteer Kansas Infantry during the Civil War, he took a job hunting buffalo to supply railroad workers with meat.

Shooting North America's largest land mammal from the back of a galloping horse was as difficult as it was dangerous. Bison can weigh over two tons, and a stampeding herd raised a massive dust cloud that made it impossible to avoid holes and other hazards. But Cody was a natural: he claimed 4,280 kills in 18 months, most using a .50 caliber Springfield rifle he named Lucretia Borgia. This broke all previous records and earned him the nickname he would carry to worldwide fame: Buffalo Bill.

Cody's résumé grew more extensive by the year. He worked as a scout for the U.S. 5th Cavalry, receiving the Congressional Medal of Honor for his service in 1872. In between missions, he guided famous clients like Grand Duke Alexei Alexandrovich of Russia and George Armstrong Custer on hunting trips.

His charisma and knack for promotion made the transition to show business almost inevitable. By age twenty-six, he had gained enough fame to start playing a stage version of himself in productions in the East, starting with a role in a melodrama called *The Scouts of the Prairie; or, Red Deviltry As It Is*. Audiences were hungry for anything having to do with a romanticized version of the briskly changing West, even as the messy reality was still unfolding. It was the dawn of the dime novel, inexpensive books that told sensationalized tales of outlaws, lawmen, and other denizens of the Wild West. Cody—or, more accurately, the character "Buffalo Bill" Cody—eventually starred in some 1,700 of them.

In 1883, Cody organized a traveling theatrical production that would turn him into one of the first true global superstars. Buffalo Bill's Wild West was a shelf of dime novels brought to life. It featured reenactments of famous events—Custer's Last Stand, the Pony Express, the Deadwood stagecoach—with enough grit, noise, color, and excitement to keep crowds riveted.

By the end of the nineteenth century, Buffalo Bill's Wild West had more than five hundred performers, including famed sharpshooter Annie Oakley and entire families of Native Americans. The full production, complete with bison, elk, and horses, filled eighty-two train cars. The show toured Europe and the Americas, performing for presidents, royalty, and the occasional pope, and eventually ran for almost thirty years.

Cody had lived through many of the historical events his showcase portrayed, and that firsthand experience, combined with his thespian instinct, was a formula for winning fans and making money. If doing so meant sanding away reality's rough edges so that the final product, the *entertainment*, bore only a surface resemblance to what had actually happened, so be it. Cody didn't obsess over authenticity like we might today, perhaps because he knew that achieving it was impossible— reenactment, by definition, means exiting the realm of the real.

Nonetheless, Cody saw his Wild West performances more like a living history lesson than a "show" or, God forbid, a circus. Those were real bullets in Annie Oakley's rifle and live bison in the "buffalo hunt," although those guns fired blanks. (Cody boasted, apparently without irony, that there were "not so many buffaloes on the whole American continent" as he had on display.) Some of the Lakota Sioux who performed in the dramatization of Custer's Last Stand had even taken part in the actual battle twenty-two years earlier; no wonder the performance was said to have moved Custer's widow, Elizabeth, to tears.

In the end, the (white) heroes always defeated the (Indian) villains; the stagecoach always made it through; and cowboys dazzled with their horsemanship and roping wizardry. This version of history had no drudgery, poverty, drunkenness, or disease—just wilderness and wildness tamed by the forces of civilization and progress. It was the West that audiences wanted, even dreamed about, and they couldn't get enough. Year after year, in arena after arena throughout the continent and beyond, sold-out crowds gobbled up Cody's easily digestible stories of bravery and conquest.

BY 1898, AMERICA WAS in a particularly martial mood. The Spanish-American War had raged for nearly four months over the spring and summer, with fighting from the Philippines to Guantánamo Bay. Some of the American soldiers who walked the streets of Cheyenne—and some of Cody's performers—bore battle scars from places like Manila and San Juan. Just a few weeks before

Cody opened the second Frontier Days celebrations, representatives from the United States and Spain signed a Protocol of Peace in Washington, D.C., that ended the fighting.

That same day, August 12, 1898, the Newlands Resolution came into effect, beginning the annexation process that would establish Hawaii as a U.S. territory. In contrast to the violent battles to "win" the frontier, the takeover of Hawaii was almost entirely peaceful, the end result of decades of slow-burn economic influence and political manipulation.* By the end of the 1800s, the vise of imperialism was tightening fast. Attempts to assert sovereignty, including creating a Hawaiian flag and issuing a Hawaiian currency, fell flat or were simply steamrolled by outside interests.

In the United States, advocates of expansion like Teddy Roosevelt believed it was America's time to take the lead on the global stage. "If we are to be a really great people," Roosevelt wrote, "we must strive in good faith to play a great part in the world." The particularly American blend of capitalism, democracy, and religion seemed to be working so well that it was hard for some to understand why more "backward" places *wouldn't* welcome this new and visionary formula for governance and prosperity.

Opponents of Manifest Destiny questioned the morality of taking over foreign lands and pointed out the heavy costs of administering an empire. Mark Twain, one of imperialism's

---

*Peaceful only in the sense of no armed conflict; smallpox and measles brought by outsiders killed as much as 75 percent of Hawaii's native population.

most vocal critics, imagined a future United States "returning, bedraggled, besmirched, and dishonored, from pirate raids in Kiao-Chou, Manchuria, South Africa, and the Philippines, with her soul full of meanness, her pockets full of boodle, and her mouth full of hypocrisies. Give her soap and a towel, but hide the looking-glass." Besides, if any people had an insight into the tendency of colonies to revolt, it was Americans.

In 1891, Hawaii's queen Lili'uokalani tried to give native Hawaiians the right to vote. That was one step too far for Hawaii's white businessmen, who overwhelmingly favored annexation. Under the pretense of protecting American lives and property, they organized a coup. John L. Stevens, the U.S. minister to Hawaii, was fully behind the action, writing that "the Hawaiian pear is now fully ripe and this is the golden hour for the United States to pluck it."

On January 17, 1893, 162 U.S. Marines and Navy sailors occupied 'Iolani Palace in Honolulu. One of the occupiers pried the jewels off the former king's crown and later gambled them away playing dice. Hoping to avoid violence, the queen stepped down. The only casualty of the whole overthrow was a police officer who was shot in the shoulder.

Lili'uokalani wrote to President Benjamin Harrison, pleading for him to "right whatever wrongs may have been inflicted upon us." In due time, she wrote, "the true facts relating to this matter will be laid before you, and I live in the hope that you will judge uprightly and justly between myself and my enemies." There is no record of a response. Sam Parker, John Palmer Parker's grandson and a prominent political figure in the islands, was among those who added their signatures to the queen's letter.

Over the following years, tensions grew between Hawaiian nationalists and foreigners who seemed to be almost itching for a fight. In 1893, a dozen Americans in Hawaii wrote to Sanford B. Dole, president of the American-dominated provisional government, volunteering to take up arms if necessary. But the only other violence was an abortive counterrevolution in January 1895. Several people were killed during three days of fighting, but the provisional government put down the uprising and placed the queen under house arrest in the palace for her alleged role in the plot. When a court found her guilty of treason, she had little choice but to abdicate and dissolve the monarchy to avoid further bloodshed.

The next big question in Washington was whether the United States would annex the islands. In 1897, tens of thousands of native Hawaiians signed a petition opposing annexation, which they considered illegal. Although the paniolo didn't leave the ranches to take up arms and kept working for ranch owners who were mostly white, there are clues about their feelings regarding Hawaii's political fate. Many paniolo signed the petition, including Ikua Purdy and much of the Parker Ranch crew. In the town of Hauula on Oahu, a man named George Parker (no relation to John Palmer Parker) was shown a "fine time" by local cowboys because of his support for a pro-Washington candidate: paniolo lassoed Parker and dragged him through the streets as policemen scrambled to defend him from a mob. "The cowboys rode in on their horses and with whoops, yells and lassoes proceeded to show the people that it was wise to vote the Home Rule ticket," reported the local paper.

Around the same time, well-to-do foreigners were offering

their opinions to Congress. William R. Castle, the former Hawaiian minister in Washington, declared that Americans in Hawaii "earnestly desire" annexation, as do "most thoughtful Hawaiians . . . [and] many other different nationalities." Without this foothold in the Pacific, he said, "American ideas and European enlightenment must succumb to orientalism." Events during the Spanish-American War had also convinced the U.S. military of Hawaii's strategic value for a naval base and resupply station, and the quick victory against Spain had stoked imperialist sentiment in Washington. In 1898 alone, the United States would grab the Philippines, Puerto Rico, and part of the Samoan archipelago, and assume authority over Cuba.

On August 12, 1898, a ceremony took place at 'Iolani Palace formalizing Hawaii's annexation as a territory of the United States. Most native Hawaiians stayed home, including the royal family. Anyone who ventured out wore an ilima blossom, a symbol of support for the monarchy. The Royal Hawaiian Band played "Hawai'i Pono'ī," the national anthem, as the Hawaiian flag was lowered over the palace for the last time and replaced with the Stars and Stripes.* The event epitomized the credo of Manifest Destiny—white Americans' God-given right and duty to assert dominion over everywhere west of Plymouth Rock.

THE FLAGS IN CHEYENNE snapped in a knife-edged wind as the 1898 Frontier Days showcase got under way. "The beauties of a Wy-

---

*In 1959, one final star would be added when Hawaii became the fiftieth state.

oming climate were not apprciated [*sic*] by the visitors from Colorado," wrote one local reporter, "especially the ladies who came to the celebration with no wraps and only a thin shirt waist to cover their bare arms." At least one vendor at the park was undeterred, advertising "Ice cream cones—freeze your teeth and give your tongue a sleigh ride!"

Native Americans played a major role in the festivities, thanks in large part to the sixty Sioux who came to perform with Buffalo Bill's Wild West. Ten Shoshone and ten Arapaho had also come to Cheyenne from Fort Washakie Reservation near Casper, which was home to about 2,000 men, women, and children. Early in the day, members of the three once-warring tribes met to share a peace pipe, shake hands, and exchange gifts. One of the Arapaho discovered that one of the Sioux was his uncle.

Cody's relationship with Native Americans was inconsistent. In an 1866 battle, he killed a Cheyenne warrior named Tall Bull, leader of the Dog Soldiers, the most feared of the tribes' warrior societies. Three weeks after Custer and his 7th Cavalry Regiment were annihilated at the Battle of Little Big Horn, Cody killed and scalped a Cheyenne warrior named Yellow Hair in the Battle of Warbonnet Creek in northwest Nebraska. In typical Cody style, he called it the First Scalp for Custer, and later made it a popular part of his show.

Yet Cody treated his Native American employees with a measure of respect. They had steady wages, which was no small thing at a time when tribes were languishing, even starving, on reservations. In his printed programs he tried to educate his audiences about the lives and customs of the Plains

Indians. As he massaged the narrative of aggressors and victims, Cody still tried to ensure that his "exhibitions" didn't
cross the line into mockery like the popular minstrel shows of
the time. During Frontier Days and other Wild West shows,
local tribes performed dances and ceremonies. Native Americans also competed in horse and foot races, although the prize
money was always less than what whites earned.

Still, Wild West shows were inherently one-sided and ex-
ploitative, even infantilizing. By presenting Native Americans
as the antagonists in his grand pageant of the West, Cody rein-
forced negative views held by much of white America. And he
certainly demonstrated a proprietary attitude toward his native
employees; when the Bureau of Indian Affairs decided in 1890
that tribe members couldn't leave their reservations anymore
"for exhibition purposes"—the commissioner thought performing for paying customers could have "a demoralizing tendency
and retard Indian progress"—Cody complained it would ruin
his business.

It's difficult to imagine the emotions of Native American
dancers, actors, and athletes performing at Frontier Days or
other Wild West shows and rodeos. The horrors of the Indian
Wars were barely in the past; the massacre at Wounded Knee,
South Dakota, in which the U.S. 7th Cavalry killed some two
hundred Sioux, had occurred less than a decade earlier. Now
here they were, singing and acting out the tragedies that had
befallen their people.

Among Cheyenne's locals, the prevailing attitude toward
Native Americans was characterized by fascination, with under-
currents of titillation and contempt. "Thirty years ago a tele-

gram conveying intelligence of the approach of Indians would have caused great alarm and apprehension," wrote the *Daily Sun-Leader*. Now, however, "they were not received by enraged citizens with Winchester rifles, but by a quite curious crowd, who followed the little band up town."

While visiting Cheyenne that summer in 1898, Cody gave an interview in which he waxed on about how much Wyoming had changed since his first visit in 1858. "Little did I think forty years ago that in less than a half century I would be riding at the head of a procession with the governor of a state," he said. "Who knows or who can estimate the progress the forty future years will show?"

Yet he knew this story of "progress" was also one of loss:

> [T]here is something pathetic about the thought of these plains once so lively with the animals of frontier days and the yells of redskins being redeemed, as they call it, by civilization. It impresses one that civilization in its sweep takes not always only that which should be supplanted.

When there were no more true frontiersmen like himself left, he added, "frontier celebrations will be farcacal [*sic*] indeed."

In the meantime, though, Cody kept the shows going, while keeping an eye out for new material to freshen up the program. Hawaii's annexation gave the showman an opportunity, and in early 1899, he sent an agent to Oahu in search of paniolo and hula dancers to join his Wild West. Because Hawaii was now part of the United States, the agent guaranteed that anyone who took the job would have their passage back home paid for, "for there is no longer any chance for the government to bring them back; they being citizens of the one common country, with the government at Washington instead of Honolulu." The Hawaiian papers reported that the recruits would travel to the mainland in the spring, "when the weather will be less hard on them."

At least seven Hawaiians came to perform with Buffalo Bill's Wild West as it toured the country. One, George Makalena, was a genuine paniolo, but the group also included two women, a policeman, a customs officer, and a college student. The event program described them all as "horsemen fully meriting the high compliment of a place in Colonel Cody's Congress of Rough Riders of the World; equestrians full of nerve and dash and sure of seat, even if their accouterments seem outlandish and their methods surprisingly grotesque to continental riders and audiences."

The Hawaiians joined entertainers from eleven other countries to perform in front of audiences of tens of thousands. An account of one Wild West show in Omaha described the "Sandwich Island Rough Riders" galloping into the arena singing "Aloha 'Oe," the beloved song of farewell written by Queen Lili'uokalani. The women wore shirtwaists and long red pa'u—special split riding skirts worn during festivals—while the men were decked out in "bright-colored sections of cheap window curtaining for saddle blankets, trousers, ill-fitting and of noisome hue, coats of floor matting and a head-dress that looked like the half of a cocoanut shell with a plume plugged in."

Hawaiian newspapers said that the men looked *hila hila*, embarrassed. For their part, the Hawaiians said they were treated well, although they wouldn't mind better costumes and more time in front of the audience.

In 1893, just months after the overthrow of Hawaii's monarchy, the World's Columbian Exhibition in Chicago featured a Hawaii showpiece organized by white settlers pushing for annexation. Their goal was to attract even more whites to move to the islands. Visitors walked into the crater of Kilauea, complete with colored lights, "bombs and crackers," and "a hissing, bubbling sea of lava."

The Hawaii exhibit also included the first hula dancing ever seen on the mainland. Jennie Kapahu, one of the two dancers, went to Chicago despite friends' and neighbors' disapproval of her decision to share the hula with the outside world. The group continued on to Europe, performing for Kaiser Wilhelm, the czar of Russia, and other royalty. ("They looked brave and big in their uniforms," Jennie said. "But when I looked into their eyes, I could tell they were unhappy. They needed a lot of Hawaiian aloha. I felt sorry for them.") Kapahu faced more criticism for her decision when she returned to Hawaii. Her white fiancé's mother forbade him to marry a hula dancer, and whites made offensive comments wherever she walked, even to church. One day she struck back, whacking a rude *haole* over the head with her umbrella.*

---

*Performers may have been the most visible Hawaiians on the mainland, but by the turn of the century there were others scattered around North America. Hawaiians worked whaling ships and trapped furs for the Hudson's Bay Company, and herded sheep in Washington's San Juan Islands.

LIKE CODY, THE ORGANIZERS of Frontier Days understood the draw of new offerings and frequently experimented with novel events as the show became a regular annual festival. Some were flops. There was wild buffalo riding and team calf branding, with ten calves released at once pursued by twenty men. In the words of one witness, "first pair to get smoke from burning hair won." The highlight of the contest one year was when a cowboy holding a branding iron tried to mount a horse: "When he went to get on, he dabbed the iron on his horse's shoulder and got bucked off and lit on his iron, seat first, much to the delight of everybody." Other gimmicks didn't stand the test of time either, like the Gymkhana race, in which riders alternated galloping on horseback with lighting cigars, opening umbrellas, and turning their coats inside out. One year they even tried "man roping," with a rider pursuing another around the half-mile track while trying to lasso him.

Nevertheless, word spread among cowboys in Wyoming and beyond that there was real money to be won at Frontier Days. For a ranch hand making $30 to $40 a month, trying to save up for a $6 pair of boots, a $50 prize was a windfall.

Visitors from as far away as Europe arrived in Cheyenne, walked under a huge festival arch of flowers and flags, and were greeted by huge moving images projected onto a canvas hung on the side of a bank. Men from the Selig Polyscope Company showed two dozen black-and-white "flickers," including films of rolling trains and the view from a hot air balloon. Motion pictures were still so new and captivating that thousands crammed in close to watch blurry scenes they could easily see in the real world: bucking broncos, cattle milling in corrals, and stagecoach holdups.

In the evenings, every street corner had some kind of vendor or tout: a magician selling soap, a vendor of false mustaches, a blind man singing patriotic songs. Revelers tooted tin horns and whooped as cowboys in spotless white chaps and brightly colored silk shirts strode about with an "awkward, stiff-legged gait that seems forever hampered by imaginary spurs," as *Leslie's* reported. After months with only animals and one another for company, cowboys were thrilled to be out and about, attending masquerade balls and dancing to brass bands playing popular new tunes like "Shy Ann":

> *Shy Ann, Shy Ann, hop on my pony*
> *There's room here for two, dear*
> *But after the ceremony*
> *We'll both ride back home, dear, as one*
> *On my pony, from old Cheyenne*

But the scene was not always so cosmopolitan and civilized. The Cheyenne sheriff had to appoint dozens of special deputies during Frontier Days to keep an eye out for pickpockets and con men. One year the carousing visitors got particularly rowdy, "turning over the stands of hawkers and engaging in other deviltry." After midnight they found the gutters full of doughnuts and rolls that food-stand workers had tossed out when they closed. "These were converted into missile[s] by the crowd and were soon flying in every direction, to the detriment of hats and clothing."

Despite the closing and commodification of the frontier, the West was still wild. Danger and brutality still lurked beneath the sheen of modernization—and sometimes made appearances at Frontier Days. One of the competitors in the riding and roping events of August 1902 was a forty-year-old cowpuncher named Tom Horn. Horn was six foot two, with "a head that would have elected a congressman, except for a pair of deep set black beady eyes," in the words of one cowboy. He worked as a prospector, rancher, Pinkerton detective, and army scout. Horn's ruthlessness drew him into Wyoming's ongoing range wars, where he worked as a hired gun.

By 1901, Horn had already been linked to several murders. "Killing is my specialty," he once said. "I look at it as a business proposition, and I think I have a corner on the market." Horn's past finally caught up with him one drunken night in Cheyenne in January 1902. A deputy U.S. marshal got Horn to admit he had killed a fourteen-year-old sheepherder with a rifle from three hundred yards away, calling it "the best shot that I ever made and the dirtiest trick that I ever done."

Horn was still a free man when Frontier Days came in August. When word spread that he was going to compete, a local cowboy said the news "got a lot of town people out just to see if the phantom Horn was real and what he looked like." (His performance in the steer-roping contest was lackluster.)

Later that year, in one of the early West's most infamous

trials, a jury found Horn guilty of murder. He briefly escaped the Cheyenne jail by overpowering a guard, but was quickly recaptured and eventually led to the gallows. At Horn's request, two cowboys sang "Life's Railway to Heaven" before the trap-door opened.

Horn swung for seventeen minutes before dying.

Kamehameha I
(Bishop Museum)

Captain George Vancouver
(National Portrait Gallery)

John Palmer Parker,
founder of Parker Ranch
(Parker Ranch Archives)

On a visit to Hawaii in the late 1950s, photographer Ansel Adams was captivated by the landscapes of Parker Ranch. At its peak, the ranch covered 300,000 acres on Hawaii. *(Ansel Adams Publishing Rights Trust)*

Archie Kaʻauʻa about to lead a "treed" wild
bullock down the slope of Mauna Kea in 1906
(Sam Low)

Driving cattle into the surf was the final step before loading them onto
ships. *(Bishop Museum)*

ABOVE: (L–R) Paniolo Ikua Purdy, Archie Kaʻauʻa,
and Willie Spencer *(Bishop Museum)*

LEFT: Eben Low
(North Hawaiʻi Education and Research Center)

ABOVE: Paniolo were
featured on Hawaiian
currency printed in 1895.

LEFT: Lowering the
Hawaiian flag over ʻIolani
Palace during the
annexation ceremony on
August 12, 1898
*(Hawaii State Archives /
Photograph by Frank Davey)*

RIGHT: Rodeo star Bill Pickett was famous for "bulldogging": taking down a bull using only his teeth. *(Wyoming State Archives)*

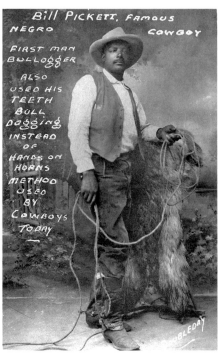

LEFT: Trailblazing bronco rider Bertha Kaepernick *(Wyoming State Archives)*

Angus MacPhee, *left (Denver Public Library)*

ABOVE: Buffalo Bill's Wild West show in 1907
(Wyoming State Archives)

LEFT: Dick Stanley at Frontier Days in 1909, before his true identity was discovered
(Wyoming State Archives)

Steer roping was one of the most popular events at Frontier Days.
(Wyoming State Archives)

ABOVE: Theodore Roosevelt presided over the opening ceremonies of Frontier Days in 1910. *(WyomingTalesandTrails.com)*

LEFT: The *Cheyenne Daily Leader*'s special 1908 Frontier Days issue

BELOW: In the wild bronco race, each contestant had to saddle his own mount before riding around the track.

8510. Cowboy Race with Wild Bronchos, Frontier Day, Cheyenne, Wyo.

Ikua Purdy tying his first steer at Frontier Days, 1908 *(Wyoming State Archives)*

The Honolulu *Sunday Advertiser* carried news of the paniolo's victory.

HAWAIIAN COWBOYS WIN HONORS AT THE CHEYENNE CONTEST

Purdy Defeats All Comers---Kaaua Takes the Third Place and Jack Low Shows Up Among First Six.

(Cablegram to Hind, Rolph & Co.)

CHEYENNE, Wyoming, August 22.—Purdy, of Hawaii, won the world's steer roping championship at the Frontier Day contest here today. His time was fifty-six seconds. Archie Kaaua took third place and Jack Low sixth.

First, third and sixth places taken by the three representatives from the Hawaiian Islands in the roping contests at Cheyenne yesterday is a record to make every Hawaiian feel proud of the plucky cowboys who traveled across the ocean to the dusty plains of Wyoming to uphold the honor of their native land.

From the brief cablegram above it is shown that Ikua Purdy defeated all comers, throwing his steer in fifty-six seconds; Archie Kaaua was third, and

ALOHA, PURDY.

From the sun-dried plains of Texas
From the rolling Northern lands,
From East and West they sent their best,
With chap and spur and flying vest,
And lariats in their hands.

From o'er the world came champions,

IKUA PURDY---Champion Steer Roper of the world. On his right is ARCHIE KAAUA, who took third place yesterday in the roping contest at Cheyenne, Wyoming. On his left is SPENCER, another expert Hawaiian cowboy.

Ikua Purdy later in life *(Billy Bergin)*

(L–R) Archie Ka'au'a, Eben Low,
Ikua Purdy *(Ka'au'a Collection)*

A statue in Waimea, Hawaii, commemorates Ikua's legend. *(Julian Smith)*

8

THE RIDER

HUNCHED LOW IN THE saddle, the paniolo spurred his horse down the narrow forest path. Mud sprayed from galloping hooves as the rider leaned from side to side to avoid being lashed by ferns and koa branches.

There are moments in the life of a cowboy when speed is everything. This was one of those times. It was May 1892, and nineteen-year-old Ikua Purdy was racing toward a small town on the coast some thirty miles away. Five miles behind him and another half mile up Mauna Kea, his cousin Eben Low was bleeding to death.

Like his grandfather, Ikua had the wiry and powerful body of a featherweight fighter. He had large brown eyes and dark hair. His hat was turned up in front in the vaquero style, which was now the style of the paniolo. He wore a bandanna around his neck, and his boots were tucked into stirrups covered with leather tapaderos.

As the crow flies, riding straight north would have been the fastest way to get to the plantation town of Honokaa. But the undulating landscape of the mountain flanks, carved into deep gulches by torrents of rock and rain, made a high-speed traverse impossible. Instead, Ikua had to ride northeast, almost directly downhill toward the Pacific Ocean. There he would follow the rough cart road along the coast to Honokaa, where he hoped to find a doctor and bring him back in time to save Eben.

Ikua dashed through sweeping grasslands for the first few miles before he entered thick forest. Gritty soil and mud gave his horse decent purchase, at least compared with the ankle-busting lava fields elsewhere on the island. The climate on the north side of Hawaii varied between punishing heat and cold. Fog and blowing mist often engulfed riders. Even when visibility was clear, there were other obstacles to contend with. Trails deteriorated into faint and splintering footpaths, overgrown with berry bushes and ferns, as they flowed from the uplands to the forests below. Paniolo horses like Ikua's were accustomed to galloping downhill, but hazards like stumps, mud pits, and downed logs lurked everywhere.

Ikua knew that if anything went wrong—if he was thrown, if his mount stumbled and injured itself, or if he was simply too slow—Eben wouldn't make it.

TWO DAYS EARLIER, IKUA, Eben, and six other cowboys had ridden out at dawn to hunt wild cattle. "Rawhide Ben" had led the party of crack ropers, including his brother Jack, his half brother Archie Kaʻauʻa, and their cousin Ikua. They rode in silence as sunrise swallowed the last few stars, a winding procession like a train of ghosts.

At twenty-eight, Eben was like an older brother to the men,

especially Ikua, who grew up emulating Parker Ranch cowboys who had worked with his father and uncles. Eben's expert riding and roping, combined with his magnetism and entrepreneurial drive, made him a natural leader. That particular week in the summer of 1892—only months before the overthrow of the Hawaiian monarchy—Eben had secured a contract to deliver animals to a cattle dealer on the coast for $7 a head.

The first day of the hunt was a tiring success. The group captured a number of young bulls, cows, and heifers, but the men also had their share of falls and near falls, stumbling over logs or getting thrown when a horse slipped or cut sideways. They returned to camp, a crude but snug cabin at 6,500 feet on the northeast slope of the mountain. They spread out their bedrolls and made sure the horses were well fed for the next day's work.

After coffee at three A.M. the next morning, they were off again, breathing clouds into the thin, cold air. The trail through the forest was so crowded with vegetation that the men had to ride single file. When the rising sun gave enough light, Eben rode to the top of a rocky outcrop to scout the terrain. This was often his favorite moment of the hunt: seated on a trusted horse and staring out over the landscape he loved, he listened for the sounds of wild cattle and mapped a plan of action in his mind.

But Eben's enthusiasm was tempered by the absence of his brother. Jack Low had refused to leave the cabin that morning. Although Jack wasn't as ebullient as his brother, he was a fast and fearless rider, and in Eben's opinion as skilled a roper as any of the men.

The night before, Jack had a dream in which someone in the family was in danger of being hurt or killed. When the cowboys woke to prepare for the day's ride, Jack was convinced that the only way he could keep this premonition from coming true was by not roping that day. The Low brothers prided themselves on being practical, can-do cattlemen, not prone to superstition. Yet hearing his brother share his dream, even at the risk of teasing from the others, made Eben decide not to push the matter. He and the others would ride without Jack for the day and reconnect with him after sunset.

The paniolo worked their way into the gullies and hidden thickets, where they could hear the soft bellowing of the animals. Eben, Ikua, and Archie soon came upon three large black bulls and immediately gave chase. Eben was about to pitch his lariat when his horse stumbled in a hog hole, left by a wild pig rooting for dinner.

Horse and rider went down in a heap, but neither were hurt. Another rider managed to rope the bull. Ikua and Archie, to no one's surprise, each captured a bull of their own. They tied the animals to trees while the riders went back to the cabin for a rest. Then it was out again to track some more.

That afternoon, one rider captured a large cow that gave Eben an uneasy feeling. The raging animal had charged the cowboys, rushing with such unexpected speed that she almost got one man.

Calculating risk was part of the job: paniolo tried to avoid taking unnecessary chances that could lead to accidents, but they needed a good haul. This time, instead of tying the unruly bullock to a tree and having to ride back uphill for it later, they decided to run it straight down to a paddock near the cabin.

Eben took responsibility for leading the animal, which had already tripped and fallen once on a rope that one of the men had let slack. He double-checked his saddle and made sure his lariat was looped around the cow's neck and the other end tied firmly to his saddle horn.

The moment the cow got to its feet, it charged him. But the paniolo was ready. He spurred his horse down the path toward the paddocks with the bullock in pursuit, leading it exactly where he wanted it to go. Galloping downhill with the furious cow behind him, Eben held his reins and lariat loosely in his right hand. With the other he quickly coiled the excess rope to take up any hoof-tangling slack.

Eben worked hard to keep the cow close to his left flank, taking in and teasing out rope. The goal was to give the animal just enough of a sense of imminent vengeance that it kept coming, without letting it get near enough to succeed—all while looking back over his shoulder and guiding the racing horse with his knees.

Horse and bullock thundered down the slope. Suddenly the bullock bolted to the right, crossing behind the horse. Just then a tree flashed past to Eben's right.

As rawhide hissed through his fingers, Eben saw the hazard in an instant. The lasso tied to the saddle horn led around his left side to the cow—which was about to pass on the far side of the tree.

When the rope ran out, Eben would be cut in half.

Instinct took over. There was no time to untie or cut the

rope. Eben hauled on the reins and jammed his left knee into the horse's flank, veering it to the right. He took the sudden slack and threw the rawhide over his head from left to right.

The maneuver likely saved his life. But in the confusion, Eben's left hand fell between the saddle horn and the rope. At that moment, the rope ran out.

It felt like his horse had been struck by lightning. Jolted by the impact, the huge bullock flew off its feet and flipped three times in midair. The rope snapped like thread.

Eben brought his startled horse to a stop, panting and blowing. He looked down at his left arm and saw nothing but pink and red. Blood was starting to pour from the mangled flesh. Shock blotted out the pain at first.

The other cowboys were off their mounts in a flash. One set to work tying a bandanna to slow the bleeding. They were about five miles from a bare-bones cabin at Hopuwai, a remote camp in an open plain that was often pummeled by cold winds blowing up from the coast. Eben insisted he could make it there on horseback. He cradled his arm and remembered Jack's premonition. Already the adrenaline was wearing off and the hurt was taking hold. He needed medical attention, but it would have to come to him.

Before they left for Hopuwai, the paniolo had to send someone for help. There was little or no discussion of who it would be; a quick nod may have been all it took. Ikua knew the braided trails, landmarks, shortcuts, and hazards of Hawaii's high country better than anyone. And he was *fast*.

As the group began a slow ride to the cabin with their injured leader, Ikua took off racing toward the coast.

———

GROWING UP ON PARKER RANCH, Ikua spent his childhood riding horses and hunting wild pigs. By age ten, he was already working alongside the Parker Ranch cowboys, and like Eben, he was tracking and roping wild cattle by his teen years. His saddle was a gift from the Parkers, who served as quasi-godparents to him and so many other ranch hands.

By the late 1800s, the Parker Ranch covered about 300,000 acres, with an estimated 25,000 head of cattle. John Palmer Parker's son, John Jr., co-managed the ranch with his nephew Sam. Unlike his uncle and grandfather, Sam Parker preferred a playboy lifestyle. Mānā had always served as a meeting place and rest stop for travelers crossing the island, much like the Hawaiian archipelago was for Pacific sailors. Sam continued that tradition, but with an aristocratic twist. He turned Mānā into a getaway for the rich and famous, surrounding the humble New England–style saltbox building with manicured gardens, ornate fountains, and outbuildings for guests and workers.

But there was nothing fancy about life on the range. Paniolo took care of livestock and maintained the ranch, with little or no interest in the social comings and goings at Mānā. Still, the ranch was more than just a place to work. It was an entire community in miniature, with housing, medical care, food, education, and venues for dances and weekend activities like baseball games. Wranglers on Hawaii's great ranches were family, figuratively and often literally.

The Purdys lived in a five-hundred-square-foot "cowboy cottage" in sight of the main house at Mānā. It had a small veranda, a woodstove, and hitching posts for the horses. Because Ikua was descended from celebrated paniolo, his career may have been preordained. But a cowboy could choose his specialty. Breaking horses, for example, was one of the more brutal jobs of the day, for rider as well as horse. Like the vaqueros, paniolo sometimes tied themselves to wild horses to keep from being thrown. If a horse fell and rolled, it could easily kill a man. Another breaking technique was to ride a horse into the surf along the Kohala Coast until it tired and stopped bucking. The indoor horse-breaking pen at Parker Ranch had dangerously low rafters, and paniolo sometimes smashed their heads against the wooden beams. This was no place for horse whispering: beating an animal with a two-by-four was common.

Ikua, a natural rider, wasn't interested in breaking horses. Years later, he told one of his sons that the job was something a cowboy's "whole body would remember"—in the form of injuries to knees, shoulders, and back. For him, the true art was riding and roping.

Ikua was a traditionalist, speaking Hawaiian at home and Pidgin English in public, if he spoke at all. He paid little attention to activities beyond ranch work; he once said that he just couldn't understand all the fuss people made about sports like football. The only thing outside of being a paniolo that seemed to draw him in was women. He was married twice and had fourteen children, and there were whispers of other women, of romantic rendezvous in hidden volcanic caves.

As a cowboy, Ikua was famous for his speed, not just on a horse, but also with a rope. He seemed to be able to find wild cattle by instinct, and when they bolted, Ikua would, in the words of another Waimea cowboy, "unwind like clockwork, to rope and tie like lightning." And he never seemed to miss. Despite his small stature, Ikua could throw a giant loop as much as forty-five feet through the air while riding at full speed. To other cowboys, it looked like he was trying to rope an elephant. Yet everything about the way he rode, threw, and worked was smooth, intuitive. As Eben put it, "We never saw a cooler man in action."

Once, when Ikua's granddaughter was a child, she and a cousin were sitting on a fence watching hundreds of cattle stampede past. The cousin slipped and fell forward into the herd. Before he could be trampled, Ikua appeared as if out of nowhere, riding at full speed. He leaned down and, without slowing, scooped the boy up and plunked him on the saddle in front of him.

And of course there was his affinity for tangling with wild cattle. One technique he was known for reminded observers of bullfighting with a lasso. When a bullock charged, Ikua kept his horse perfectly still, holding the lariat in a light loop by his side as gently as a bouquet of flowers. At the last second, he spurred the horse out of the way and dropped the loop over the bullock's head. The horse stood firm, and the shock of the rope's coming tight jerked the animal off its feet.

If the stunned bullock got up for another charge, Ikua was already moving, angling closer to create enough slack to entangle the animal again. With a roll of his wrist, he sent a loop spiraling down the lasso like a curling wave. The widened lasso wrapped around the furious bullock's legs. Before it could step out of the loop, Purdy spurred his horse in the opposite direction, leaning far out of the saddle to counterbalance the sudden yank of the animal being thrown off its feet.

He also carried a rifle for hunting, but rarely, if ever, a pistol. He once told a reporter that "only show-off cowboys carry guns."

For Ikua, running cattle was all he knew and all he ever wanted to do. "Day and night, day and night, I work on the ranch, on the range, in the saddle," he said. "No time to worry, nobody bothering you about small things. That's the life." Sometimes, if he hadn't gotten his fill by day, Ikua would go out to rope wild cattle in the moonlight, just for sport.

Yet Ikua wasn't all business. Unlike John Palmer Parker or Eben, who claimed to avoid alcohol, Ikua enjoyed a tot of gin around a campfire. He was known to crack his whip at other cowboys if they happened to be gunning for the same animal. And he had the same quiet sense of humor his father and grandfather were known for. He liked to joke that his *hapa haole* (mixed ancestry) complexion resulted from a courtship that took place in the moonlight.

In many ways, Ikua was the archetypal cowboy: outwardly humble, inwardly confident, and ultra-competent. Up before dawn, back after dark, he preferred to do the work himself rather than delegate. Aside from their shared love for life on the range, Ikua and Eben were near opposites.

WITHIN AN HOUR OF leaving Eben's side, Ikua entered a primordial forest. In 1790, Kamehameha I had marched his troops down these same trails during his conquest of the island. Some believed this ancient highway was haunted by spirits traveling to the Lua o Milu, the underground home of the dead, in the nearby Waipio Valley.

Weaving between ridges and jagged rock formations, Ikua passed 'ōhi'a trees standing like sentries, adorned with red, yellow, and golden blossoms. The harmonica-like call of the 'i'iwi bird echoed through the humid forest.

He emerged onto swaying fields of sugarcane, part of the plantations on the east side of Mauna Kea. Finally he found the path to the cart road that circumscribed much of the island.

Back at the camp, Eben was in agony, yet alert enough to know that if help didn't come soon, gangrene would.

Ikua arrived in Honokaa near sunset, filthy and exhausted, to find the local doctor was away on a maternity call. But there was a Japanese doctor who lived in the village of Kukuihaele, seven miles farther up the coast. Ikua climbed on his horse and set off again.

He reached Kukuihaele around nine P.M., found the doctor, and hurriedly helped him prepare a horse to ride up the mountain. The forty-five-mile trip took them all night and the better part of the morning. By the time they arrived at Hopuwai, Ikua had been on the move for close to thirty-two hours.

As they approached the cabin, the men could hear cries of pain. The doctor gave Eben a shot of morphine, but he could see that gangrene had set in already. They had to move him to Mānā, thirty miles away, where he could be seen by an experienced surgeon.

After the doctor bandaged Eben's wrist and what remained of his hand, the group set off again on horseback. The wounded cowboy had trouble staying upright in the saddle. During one rest break, Eben dismounted and nearly fainted in the shade of a tree. A serving of poi (pounded taro paste) helped revive him, and he somehow made it through the rest of the ride to Mānā.

Meanwhile, another cowboy had raced to a ranch that had a telephone to call a doctor named Weddick, a friend of Eben's. But when Weddick got on the line, it was clear, as one of the paniolo later put it, that he was "drunk as a boiled owl." Nevertheless, a group of wranglers loaded the man and his medical tools into a horse-drawn wagon and began the thirty-five-mile journey to Mānā. Halfway across the Kohala Mountains, the doctor emerged from his stupor and asked "what in the hell they were trying to do to him." When the cowboy told him what had happened, he "sobered up double quick" and demanded they go even faster.

By the time Weddick arrived at Mānā, Eben's hand was too far gone to save. The doctor waited for the morning light to ready his patient for amputation. He anesthetized Eben, most likely with ether, and sterilized his scalpel and bone saw.

A blacksmith and a cowboy volunteer tended to the tools and buckets of boiling water. To remove the damaged hand, the doctor had to cut through the remaining tissue and saw through the bone where the wrist met the forearm. In the next room, Eben's brother Jack wept.

Considering the tropical climate, the threat of infection, and the ad hoc surgical suite, the procedure went remarkably smoothly. Over the next three weeks, Weddick provided Eben with ample opiates to help counter the intense pain. Weddick

later said Eben was as "strong as a steer," and that a less hearty
patient surely would have died.

After his arm healed, Eben learned to ride and rope again
with just one hand, eventually outperforming most men who
still had two. His method—holding the reins and lariat coils in
his left elbow and throwing with his right hand—was remarkably effective; he once roped and tied a steer one-handed in fifty-
two seconds. Eben also came to realize that his disability could
be an asset, a promotional tool even better than the moniker
Rawhide Ben. Being the best one-handed cowboy in the islands
meant serious bragging rights.

Even then, Eben knew, as did many of his fellow Waimea
Boys, that the best paniolo they'd ever seen was the one who
had just saved his life.

9

COWBOY KING OF THE ISLANDS

THE GUARD WITH A sawed-off Winchester across his lap sat on the front seat of the rolling stagecoach, eyes alert for trouble. Even so, the small party of pioneers inside never stood a chance. A group of mounted Indians was lying in ambush, waiting for just the right moment.

With piercing war cries, the braves gave chase, and the sounds of the ensuing gunfight echoed up and down the beach. They soon overtook the coach, disarmed the guard, and bound their captives. The attackers rifled through the victims' belongings and made preparations to dispatch the God-fearing homesteaders. Then, just when all seemed lost, a group of U.S. cavalrymen arrived to deliver a thunderous counterattack. Clouds of gunpowder smoke filled the tropical air, the Indians fled, and the thankful captives were saved.

The dramatized stagecoach holdup was exemplary Wild West theater, and the spectators gathered that afternoon in December of 1905 at Honolulu's Kapi'olani Park ate it up. Early twentieth-century Hawaii, like much of the world, was caught up in frontier fever.

Shows popularized by Buffalo Bill Cody had conquered the Americas and Europe, spreading an image of the West that was so vivid, so specific, that even people living an ocean away had little patience for imitators. A performance in Honolulu a few years earlier received scathing criticism before it even opened. The papers warned that the show would deliver a hippodrome without chariots and a Wild West show without American Indians—little more than "a circus tent and a few shabby costumes." The inauthenticity reeked. Apparently the event's organizer "imagines Honolulu people are not aware of this fact—but they are."

As Isabella Bird had seen during her visit in the 1870s, riding had become enormously popular in the islands, even outside the world of the paniolo. Hawaiians rode for transportation and fun, swinging polo mallets on grassy fields and racing any-where there was room. On June 11, 1872, horse racing was part of the festivities at the Kamehameha Day holiday celebration. The Hawaiian Jockey Club was established that same year, and soon racetracks, like the one at Kapiʻolani Park on the edge of Waikiki Bay, had been cleared on patches of flat ground throughout the islands.

It was only natural that Hawaiians wanted to see pani-olo compete in riding and roping contests. An early example, from 1896, was billed as an "Amusement Carnival," with ads promising "scenes in the wild west" on a baseball field in Ho-nolulu. Other horse-racing events began to feature "bona fide cowpunchers." The Jockey Club usually hosted races for club members only, but in 1902 it held a three-mile relay race for cowboys, although "natives" were encouraged to participate.

That winter, employees of island ranches competed against one another in contests held on New Year's Day. (Parker Ranch paniolo had taken up a collection for the prize money.)

Hilo's 1903 Fourth of July festivities included horse races and a cowboy tournament that was one of the first demonstrations of roping and bronco riding in Hawaii. The controlled setting was a far cry from the rugged slopes of Mauna Kea; the "fretful cows and steers" were enclosed in a corral in the middle of the field. Yet work on the ranches was so unfamiliar to most island residents that even a small demonstration of paniolo skill was real entertainment. The local papers described in detail how each homegrown cowboy, with the "swish of the lariat" and a "clever turn," had his steer down and tied prostrate in no time.

There was an unavoidable irony to Hawaiians celebrating the Fourth of July so soon after annexation. More than half of Hawaii's native and mixed-race residents opposed the new government. For many of them, celebrating America's birthday must have been like throwing a party for your own kidnapper. Adding to the incongruity was the fact that compared with the segregated United States, Hawaii, while hardly a post-racism utopia, was in many ways a more harmonious and progressive place. By 1900, the islands' population of roughly 154,000 was almost 20 percent Hawaiian, 40 percent Japanese, 7 percent Caucasian, 17 percent Chinese, 11 percent Portuguese, and 5 percent part Hawaiian—far more diverse than the rest of the United States, which was almost 90 percent white, and with far less racial violence and persecution. Hawaii was the melting pot that America, at least on paper, aspired to be.

For paniolo, Fourth of July competitions were a chance to take a break from the relentless work and responsibilities on the ranch. They could test themselves against one another and maybe make a bet or two on the side; as the old cowboy saying went, "Rodeo is borned of brags." In the eyes of management, such contests were preferable to other diversions. Despite the modest wages of a cowboy, hanging around in Waimea meant tempting trouble. Parker ranch manager A. W. Carter knew that drunkenness was rife in the town—even the deputy sheriff and his officers were often soused. Carter tried to make Waimea a dry town by convincing a judge to revoke the liquor license of at least one establishment and spying on his men to make sure they weren't getting drunk. He even considered opening a Parker Ranch store and restaurant for the specific purpose of driving other liquor-based operations out of business, but he ultimately decided against it.

FAR FROM ENDING HIS career, losing a hand had boosted Eben's reputation as one of the toughest riders in the islands. His joie de vivre survived intact. He liked to surprise new acquaintances by tossing his prosthetic hand into their laps, causing more than a few horrified screams. Once, after a bearded cowboy fell asleep on the porch at Eben's home, Eben collected burs from the tails of horses and delicately entangled them in the man's beard.

Eben's wife, Elizabeth Napoleon, grew up in Honolulu, not far from ʻIolani Palace, but she adjusted well to life in Hawaii's high country. Lizzie wore her hair in a braid under a Stetson hat and, according to Eben, was "an excellent horsewoman, a crack shot, and a perfect companion all of the time."

Lizzie's upbringing and worldview left her at odds with many of her contemporaries. Her mother, Pamaho'a, was related to the royal family and thus an unabashed supporter of the monarchy. But when Lizzie was about thirteen, she was sent to live with Sanford B. Dole and his wife, who had no children of their own. This arrangement, known as *hānai,* is an informal form of adoption in Hawaiian culture, meant to help cement interfamily connections and share the joy of caring for children.

Dole, a close friend of Eben's, would go on to become the point person for the group of American businessmen and pro-U.S. politicians who orchestrated the overthrow of Hawaii's monarchy, and he served as the newly established territory's first governor.* Lizzie embraced her adopted parents' view that Hawaii was better off under the wing of the United States, and this put her at odds with most Hawaiians, including her mother.

In Eben, however, Lizzie had an unwavering ally. They both supported annexation and felt that Hawaiians should focus on the future instead of mourning the past. Lizzie told her daughter, Clorinda, that when it came to schooling and speech: "You are going to live in a haole world. You had better learn how to be [haole]." The Low children were forbidden to speak Hawaiian, even though Eben and Lizzie spoke it fluently. (Clorinda later said her parents would speak Hawaiian only when they didn't want the children to know what they were saying.)

---

*His cousin James founded the Hawaii Pineapple Company, the precursor of today's multinational colossus Dole Food.

On Hawaii, the Lows hosted all-night parties at Puʻuwaʻawaʻa, the ranch twenty miles southwest of Waimea that Eben co-owned with a business associate. Sanford Dole was a frequent guest, as were many prominent loyalists. It was an interesting mix, and further evidence of the civility that underscored life in the islands, even among political adversaries. Puʻuwaʻawaʻa was a place where Eben and Lizzie's wide circle of friends could gather to hunt, drink, and relax.

But financial problems haunted Eben during the first years of the new century. Pinched between creditors and tight margins, he struggled to keep Puʻuwaʻawaʻa afloat. In 1902 he was finally forced to sell his stake in the ranch.

During this same period, a simmering dispute over control of Parker Ranch intensified. Eben, together with his brother Jack and John Palmer Parker's grandson Sam, felt they should be running the now-famous spread. They were family, after all. Instead, operations were overseen by A. W. Carter, a Honolulu lawyer with a longtime interest in ranching. Carter had been appointed guardian and trustee of John Palmer Parker's five-year-old great-great-granddaughter, Thelma. Thelma had inherited half ownership of the estate in 1894, after the sudden death of her father. Carter had moved to Waimea and proved to be a gifted and dedicated steward of the ranch, but Sam Parker and the Lows felt they could do better, and were in fact the rightful heirs to the estate. The quarrel grew ugly, with the Low brothers and Sam Parker trying repeatedly to wrest control of the ranch from Carter.

A low point of the Parker Ranch saga took place in June 1904. Eben was in Waimea, trying to enlist paniolo to support him, Jack, and Sam in their takeover campaign. The cowboys weren't buying it, and they advised Eben to seek justice through the legal system. One day Eben marched into Carter's office armed with six-shooters and tried to strong-arm the lawyer into signing over control of the ranch. Carter stood his ground and Eben left, abandoning his extralegal effort for good. A Honolulu court eventually dismissed the lawsuit.

If Lizzie was caught between royalists and those supporting America's provisional government, Eben was caught between the workaday cowboys and Hawaii's aristocrats. He was a true paniolo who traced his lineage back to Kamehameha I. Sure, he hammed it up with pistols and polished boots. But he was also a bona fide member of a tight community of unpretentious cowboys, most of whom favored Hawaiian independence.

At the same time, Eben saw himself as part of the upper echelon of Hawaiian society, with aspirations beyond a simple life in the saddle. He liked to mingle with wealthy business owners, well-connected families, and other power brokers in Honolulu. His friendship with Dole, his support of annexation, and even the fact that he forbade his children to speak Hawaiian at home were all evidence of a man conflicted.

Instead of letting himself be dragged down by Hawaii's political turmoil or his own compounding losses—his hand, Puʻuwaʻawaʻa, Parker Ranch—Eben threw himself into all manner of schemes and businesses. While still working cattle on Hawaii, he spearheaded ventures ranging from shipwreck salvage to a homing pigeon messaging service. He guided visitors up Mauna Kea and was so concerned about the dire state of Hawaii's native forests that he had woodpeckers imported from the mainland, in the hope that they would eat disease-carrying insects. (They didn't.) He worked for a time in the shipping business and even tried his hand as an arts promoter, booking events for Hawaiian dancers and singers.

Eben finally found his calling and made the biggest impact as the self-styled ambassador for Hawaii's ranches and champion of paniolo culture. In the winter of 1903, he donned a narrow-brimmed hat and, together with Lizzie, sailed to the West Coast, first arriving in San Francisco to visit with friends. After Eben delivered a speech to the National Livestock Producers Association convention in Portland, Oregon, he and Lizzie traveled to North Texas to learn about local ranching and feeding methods. The Texans were quite taken with the one-handed cowboy and his tales and photos of Hawaii's ferocious bullocks. After Eben gave a presentation showing cattle being herded into the surf, *The Dallas Morning News* concluded that "Texas ranching is rather tame" in comparison.

They then headed east to New Orleans and on to Washington, D.C., where Eben dipped a toe in politics by telling local reporters he thought Hawaii should have more autonomy. In an interview, he argued that a set of sweeping controls President Roosevelt wanted to grant U.S. representatives in Hawaii would lead to abuses of power that contradicted the same democratic ideals used to justify overthrow of the monarchy. He may have been friends with Dole and supported annexation, but Eben didn't want to see Hawaii infantilized, either.

In January 1904, Eben went to the White House to drop in on the president. He carried a letter from Hawaii's governor introducing him as "one of the best cowboys on the island of

Hawaii"—wording Eben himself may have suggested. As Eben later recalled, he waited in the anteroom while a clerk struggled to figure out who he was and what race he was. Fed up with the "hemming and hawing," Eben called out: "Tell Mr. Roosevelt that Rawhide Ben of Hawaii is returning his call!"

From the Oval Office, an even louder voice rang out: "Where's that cowboy? I'm delighted to meet Hawaii's famous cowboy!"

Eben had finally met his match in bravado and verbosity. When he was able to get a word in edgewise, he told Roosevelt how his island had cowhands "long before anyone heard of Wyoming."

"Say, I'd like to have you come to Hawaii," Eben added.

Roosevelt laughed. He asked whether there was any good hunting to be had out there. Eben described one of his favorite spots, a thousand-acre area of open plain not far from Pu'uwa'awa'a full of wild turkeys, geese, quail, and pheasant. He urged Roosevelt to join him on a hunt there someday, and the president said he hoped to do so.

BY THE END OF 1905, Eben was back in Honolulu, throwing his energy into organizing the biggest "Cowboy Carnival" the islands had ever seen. Some of the Parker Ranch aces were already in town; all Eben had to do was send for their horses, secure steers, feed, and other equipment from Oahu ranches, convince his friends in the polo and horse-racing world to lend him a venue, and publicize the event. As the consummate promoter, he saw this as a reasonable to-do list. If he could pull it off, the event would make a profit. Even if it didn't, it still promised to be a hell of a show.

Organizing the rodeo was a way to show off so much paniolo talent in one place. ("He was always promoting something," Eben's daughter once said.) But there may have been another motive for setting up the event. That same month, the latest chapter of the ongoing legal battle over Parker Ranch was playing out in a Honolulu courtroom. Eben had arranged for a group of paniolo from Waimea, including his cousin Ikua and half brother Archie Kaʻauʻa, to testify about Carter's mismanagement of the ranch. In orchestrating the Cowboy Carnival, Eben was likely also out to show that the Waimea Boys were *his* boys, that everyone working together under his leadership was the natural order of things, in the hopes that a certain judge in Honolulu would see it that way, too.

Whatever his motives, it's a testament to Eben's influence and drive that, after only a few weeks of preparation, the Cowboy Carnival at Kapiʻolani Park on October 21, 1905, drew one of the largest peacetime crowds the islands had ever seen. "The town has practically been turned over to the cowboys for this afternoon," reported the *Honolulu Advertiser*, "and nearly all Honolulu will be on hand to witness the merry sports of gents of the spurs and lariats."

Like Cheyenne Frontier Days, the Cowboy Carnival at Kapiʻolani blended Wild West skits, lighthearted games, and dead-serious sporting contests. (The winner of the bucking event suffered "nothing worse than a dislocated shoulder which was speedily put into commission again.") Eben pumped the press with details—the steers were "about the wildest specimens he has ever seen," he told one reporter—and gave an exhibition of one-armed roping. The papers also ran stories about the star cowpunchers, including Ikua, "said to be the champion of them all." Eben bragged that his cousin could rope and tie a steer in twenty seconds.

By the turn of the century, a basic set of rules for roping contests was widely accepted, with very little variation from place to place. In broad terms, a man on horseback tried to lasso a sprinting steer, throw it to the ground, and tie its legs together as quickly as possible. Each animal got a head start—originally as much as 150 feet, but this was shortened over time—before a waved flag signaled the rider to take off in pursuit.

As the steer bolted forward, it could weave, stop dead, or change direction on a dime while the horse thundered up behind. At the right moment, the cowboy threw a lasso at the speeding animal. If he hit his target, he tied a quick knot around his saddle horn. The second the loop settled, a well-trained horse would stop short and brace itself, snapping the rope taut and "busting" the steer off its feet.

Before the horse had even stopped, the rider had already jumped down to run at the stunned steer. A cattle-savvy horse kept the rope tight enough so the steer couldn't get back on its feet, but not so tight that it dragged the steer along the ground. The cowboy then took a short "piggin' string," held in his teeth or tucked under his belt, and whipped it around the prone steer's feet and finished with a quick knot called a hooey.* The

---

*Early contests required tying all four legs, but the rule was later changed to three.

clock stopped when the contestant threw his hands in the air to show he was done. If the animal struggled free of the rope, the attempt didn't count. In most early rodeos, each contestant had two tries, and the average of the two times constituted a final score.

During the steer-roping event that winter in Honolulu, Archie Ka'au'a scored a time of 1 minute and 33 seconds, among the day's fastest. But because he had made three throws, one more than the rules allowed, he was disqualified.

Everyone assumed Ikua would easily take the roping prize. For the past few years, the unassuming paniolo had been winning contests throughout the islands, whether it was an organized event or impromptu challenge from peers. By 1905, he was widely recognized as Hawaii's top roper, "the cowboy king of the islands," as one newspaper put it. But that day at Kapi'olani Park, a young rider from Oahu roped and tied his steer in 46 seconds. The crowd went berserk and assumed the contest was over.

They were wrong. Ikua was next. He brought his steer down with one of his famously wide loops. When he finished tying, the clock read 38.75 seconds. There's no record of Ikua's reaction, but it's hard not to think of him wearing the knowing grin of a maestro.

It was a huge moment for the Waimea Boys, Hawaii's growing community of rodeo fans, and paniolo as a whole. As the *Sunday Advertiser* wrote, "the world's record for roping and tying a four-footed animal is not many seconds less than the time made by Purdy." Soon enough, he would have a chance to test himself against the world's best.

10

A ROYAL GOOD TIME

I N THE AUTUMN OF 1907, Eben Low was back on the mainland—this time in Cheyenne.

Months of travel had taken him from Massachusetts to Los Angeles and Nevada. His final stop was Frontier Days. "They treated me royally," he later told a reporter. "I was given a marshal's badge which permitted me to go anywhere and everywhere on the grounds. Captain Hardy, champion rifle shot, and myself, palled around together and had a great time."

In Wyoming, Eben took in a show that had few equals in North America. Frontier Days had grown larger every year since its inception, adding new events, bigger prizes, and more Wild West drama. A few years earlier, one of the attendees was none other than the cowboy president himself, Theodore Roosevelt.

Roosevelt had been to Cheyenne once before, in 1900, to give a speech at the opera house as William McKinley's vice presidential candidate. In May 1903, as president, he went for fun. The city welcomed the mustachioed commander in chief like a long-lost son and arranged a special one-day show at

Frontier Park just for him. Seated in a special stand inside the track within spitting distance of the action, Roosevelt watched the events with almost childlike excitement. The wild horse race, he later recounted, was the finest riding he had ever seen. Whenever the United States needed cavalrymen in the future, he mused, "these are the men we want, for with them courage is infused by the life they lead."

A Nebraska cowboy named Clayton Danks rode a vicious bull during the showcase for the president. Danks had started competing in rodeos as a teenager, and was already being called "one of the most spectacular and perfect riders in the West." Despite the beast's best efforts to stick a horn through him, Danks stayed on.

When the day's exhibition was over, Roosevelt said his visit to Cheyenne was "as pleasant a forty-eight hours as any president ever spent since the White House was built." Danks, meanwhile, would go on to win two Frontier Days championships in the coming years.

Sitting in the stands in 1907, Eben Low watched Indians perform "scalping dances" and other demonstrations between rodeo events. Some of the same Indians appeared in town in the evenings at band concerts and masked balls. Barely a generation had passed since the last major battles of the Indian Wars: some of the people who walked the streets had likely participated, on one side or the other, in Custer's Last Stand (1876) or the Wounded Knee Massacre (1890).

Reporters covering Frontier Days noted how visitors gawked at "dignified and stoical Red Men stalking gravely along the streets, brushing shoulders with the haute ton"—high society—

"with startling sang froid." People were particularly interested in the fact that cattle injured during the rodeo were given to the tribes to butcher and turn into jerky. Yet fascination with Native Americans' eating habits didn't stop there: "If there is anything which a real live Indian likes more than whisky it is the flesh of a nice fat dog," one newspaper declared, "and after Frontier day there will be less barking about the streets at night." In an article titled "Dog Eat at Injun Camp," the *Wyoming Times* described how a white visitor took part:

> One dainty, charmingly attired young lady expressed the desire to partake of the feast . . . with a wry grimace and a series of extraordinary facial contortions, the remarkable gastronomical feat was at last accomplished and the crowd of expectant visitors were almost converted to cannibalism when to their astonishment they heard the young lady pronounce the dish delightfully palatable.

During Eben's two visits to the mainland in the early twentieth century, he was disturbed by the country's pervasive racism. "It is too bad that hurts are given and errors are made, and apologies follow, when all we have to do in our world is accept each other as people!" he wrote. "You learn to take people as they come, keeping your own dignity, your own sense of values, and being able to recognize a Real Man when you find one, colored or white." It sounded enlightened but didn't exactly mesh with how Eben and Lizzie felt about Hawaiian ways and the Hawaiian language.

In Wyoming, bigotry was no less pervasive than it was in other parts of the West. Yet women and African Americans both featured prominently—and positively—in Frontier Days' early years.

Wyoming was a women's rights pioneer from its earliest days. On the frontier, women had to shoulder many of the same responsibilities as men, whether it was navigating a wagon trail or running a ranch. In 1869, before the Wyoming Territory was even two years old, the legislature passed an unrestricted women's suffrage law, the first of its kind in the country. Allowing women to vote was partly a strategy to attract more female settlers; at the time, there was only one woman for every six men. ("We now expect at once quite an immigration of ladies to Wyoming," declared one paper. "We say to them all, come on.") But the law was also motivated by changing values: William Bright, a legislator and saloon owner in South Pass City, spearheaded the effort because he judged his wife "as good as any man and better than convicts and idiots."

The move drew a predictable backlash—from the liberal Northeast, no less. *Harper's Weekly* wrote that "Wyoming gave women the right to vote in much the same spirit that New York or Pennsylvania might vote to enfranchise angels or Martians if their legislatures had time for frivolous gaiety." Regardless, the suffrage milestones continued. In 1870, Esther Hobart Morris was appointed the country's first justice of the peace in South Pass City, 250 miles from Cheyenne. Fifty-six years old and six feet tall, Justice Morris was described as "mannish" and "lantern-jawed," and her appointment was decried as "unnatural" and "dangerous." Her first case involved prosecuting her male predecessor for refusing to turn over the court docket after he resigned in protest of the new suffrage law. The case was dismissed, the docket never delivered, and Morris bought her own.

The following spring, the first grand jury to have women members convened in Laramie. The case was a manslaughter charge relating to a barroom shooting. (The courtroom also saw America's first female bailiff.) The six women on the jury had to enter the courtroom veiled, and newspaper editorials expressed concern about the effect the experience would have on their fragile constitutions: "It will be almost a miracle if some of the delicate women who are going through this painful ordeal do not sink under the weight of their privations and return to their homes with shattered nerves and reduced health." It took the jury two days to return a verdict of guilty.

Wyoming also had relatively liberal divorce laws. Other states required women to wait up to a year before they could remarry, but in Wyoming the wait was only sixty days. In a place with so many more men than women, "grass widows" had little trouble finding another partner. It was so common for women to travel up from Denver to take advantage of the law that one of the most prominent divorce firms in the United States, New York–based Hoggatt & Caruthers, established a branch office in Cheyenne in 1899. Today, Wyoming's state motto is "Equal Rights."

ON A SOAKING WET September day in 1904, a tall figure led a horse into the arena facing the Frontier Park grandstand. Bertha

Kaepernick was twenty-two years old, "a strong husky gal of German descent," in the words of one witness, with bright brown eyes and brown hair. Rain had turned the track into a morass of mud, and the cowboys were insisting that the bucking contest be postponed because it was too dangerous. But the crowd—drenched, restless, and eager for action—booed and protested the delay until Kaepernick stepped forward.

Kaepernick had grown up on a ranch in Colorado. When she was five, her father had placed her on the back of a horse and said, "Now, Bertha, be sure you stay on board. If you get off, there may not be anyone around to put you back on." She did, and from then on it was hard to get her off a horse. She soon began competing in rodeos. At the time, cowgirls were welcome to help out on farms and ranches. But if they dared compete in what were considered the manliest of contests, cowgirls faced a deep-seated sexism that branded them "loose women" or "strenuous dames." Some even argued that bronco riding was harmful to a woman's reproductive system (yet somehow not a man's). Nevertheless they persisted, sometimes riding and roping in full-length bloomers or split riding skirts.

Annie Oakley's sixteen years of touring with Buffalo Bill's Wild West made her the most celebrated example of a woman succeeding on her own terms in an overwhelmingly male arena. When he wasn't standing frozen so his wife could shoot a cigarette out of his mouth, Oakley's husband, Frank Butler, served as her secretary and manager. Oakley advocated for women to carry guns for protection; in one newspaper article, she showed women how to hide a gun under an umbrella. By her own estimate Oakley taught 15,000 women to shoot. She also campaigned for equal pay and advocated for women to pursue an active life outside of the house, even if it involved typically "male" pursuits like shooting and riding bicycles. "I think sport and healthful exercise makes women better, healthier, and happier," she said.

At the turn of the century, the most famous woman competing in rodeos was probably Lucille Mulhall, a rider and trick roper from Oklahoma. When Mulhall was a girl, her father bet her she couldn't rope a fence post three times in a row. She did. According to one story, when Teddy Roosevelt visited her family's ranch, he bet her she couldn't lasso a coyote from horseback. She did that too, then killed it with a stirrup and gave Roosevelt the pelt.

At fourteen, Mulhall started performing in her father's Wild West show, where she was billed as the Champion Lady Steer Roper of the World. "Little Miss Mulhall, who weighs only 90 pounds, can break a bronco, lasso and brand a steer and shoot a coyote at 500 yards," wrote the *New York World*. "She can also play Chopin, quote Browning, construe Virgil and make mayonnaise dressing. She is a little ashamed of these latter accomplishments, which are a concession to the civilized prejudices of her mother." Will Rogers, astonished by her virtuosity, still couldn't resist the chauvinist take, calling her "the only girl that ever rode a horse exactly like a man."

Women had so far been forbidden from competing in Frontier Days bucking contests because, in the words of one planner, "We don't have time to haul women bronco fighters to the hospital." Organizers changed the rule in 1904, but only as a promotional gimmick; they didn't expect any women to come.

But when Kaepernick heard that she could compete, she set off alone for Cheyenne, over a hundred miles away. She followed the railroad tracks most of the way, riding one horse and leading an unbroken mount named Tombstone.

It turned out she was the only woman participating that year, but Frontier Days promoters still made hay of the news: "The real active idea of Woman Suffrage was thus demonstrated in Wyoming at a Frontier Days show," said Warren Richardson, the event's chairman.

When Kaepernick led Tombstone out onto the mucky track, spectators jumped onto their seats, cheering. Witnesses described the horse as "long, lean and lanky, [and] full of deviltry, with eyes blazing at the injustice of being burdened with such a monstrosity of a saddle." The crowd watched as Kaepernick climbed onto the horse, settled herself, and gave the signal to turn the animal loose. Tombstone spun, sidestepped, twisted, and stood on his hind legs, spraying mud in every direction. Moments later the horse reared up so high he toppled over backward, a notorious move called a "widow-maker." Spectators screamed.

But Kaepernick deftly slid to one side just before Tombstone hit the ground. Undeterred, she remounted as the horse scrambled to his feet. The audience roared with delight. In due time, Tombstone stopped and looked about, amazed. Kaepernick was still on board.

It was one of the most remarkable exhibitions of bronco riding Cheyenne had ever seen, the *Wyoming Tribune* concluded, tacking on the backhanded compliment that it still "would have been exciting had the rider been a man."

After Kaepernick's demonstration, the men had no choice but to ride in the mud. Kaepernick rode in the finals, but was disqualified because she touched the rigging with her free hand. But her effort showed what women could do in the rodeo arena, and soon the sight of a cowgirl riding a bronco or racing a pony was unremarkable.

The same year Kaepernick thrilled spectators for the first time, Frontier Days also saw one of the most daring and spectacular stunts in its history—performed by the son of a former slave.

Bill Pickett was born in the 1870s in the Texas brush country, the second of thirteen children. His father was African American and his mother was Native American. With a compact body and outsize confidence in his athletic ability, Pickett had dropped out of grade school to work as a ranch hand. He proved to be so talented with animals that he began performing at fairs and rodeos in Colorado, Arizona, and Texas.

As many as one in four cowboys in the American West was African American. Recently freed slaves and their children found that the West offered more autonomy and opportunity than the East, where racism was more entrenched and often the only jobs available were service positions like elevator operators or railroad porters. By the late nineteenth century, close to fifty all-black towns had been founded across five western states and territories. African American cowboys worked on ranches and helped with cattle drives, where they earned the same wages as whites and more than Mexicans. In a Dodge City boardinghouse, Denver saloon, or Cheyenne hardware store, a black cowboy's money was as good as anyone's.

Life on the range was hardly free of racial discrimination and persecution. Blacks were often barred from participating in rodeos, which is one reason Pickett went by the vague moniker "The Dusky Demon." Racial epithets were common in print and conversation, and African American cowboys were frequently given the hardest jobs, like handling fighting bulls and testing river crossings on cattle drives, although this may have been as much a testament to their ability as anything.

But competence was competence. Skin color meant little to ranchers who needed hardworking men to supervise their fast-growing herds, and in time a handful of African American cowboys gained a measure of fame. The former slave Nat Love, aka "Deadwood Dick," wrote a popular 1907 autobiography full of stories about winning rodeos, meeting Billy the Kid, and escaping from Pima Indians.* Al Jones, an African American driver from Texas, served as trail boss on four major cattle drives in his career, including one leading 2,000 steers in 1885. Stagecoach Mary Fields, the first black postal carrier in the United States, was said to have broken more noses than any other person in Montana. Fields smoked cigars and packed a .38 Smith & Wesson under her skirts. She also babysat local

---

*Some black cowboys had their stories recast with white protagonists. One of the models for the Lone Ranger was Bass Reeves, the first black deputy U.S. marshal west of the Mississippi. Reeves made over 3,000 arrests, including bringing in his own son on murder charges. The 1956 John Wayne film *The Searchers*, and the novel it was based on, was inspired by the story of Britt Johnson, also an African American cowboy, whose wife and two children were captured by Comanches in 1864.

children and gave flowers from her garden to baseball players whenever they hit a home run.

In Cheyenne, as in Hawaii, race relations were relatively progressive compared to the country as a whole. The Inter-Ocean Hotel, the largest in the city, had been built and managed by Barney Ford, an African American, and the city hired its first African American policeman in 1881. In the 1880s, the segregated 9th and 10th Cavalry regiments were assigned to nearby Fort Russell under Captain John "Black Jack" Pershing, who went on to command American forces on the Western Front in World War I. (Indian tribes called the African American servicemen Buffalo Soldiers for the color and texture of their hair.) Cheyenne citizens had "solemnly resolved to hate and detest the colored troops before their arrival," reported the *Daily Leader*, but the men conducted themselves so admirably that "contempt soon turned to respect."

When Pickett stepped into the Frontier Days ring in 1904, the audience was primed for something extraordinary. His signature move was called bulldogging, and it consisted of taking down a full-grown steer using only his teeth.

As a teenager, Pickett had watched trained bulldogs take down bulls: a "heel dog" went for a leg, while a "catch dog" latched onto the animal's nose or lip. He decided to try it himself, alone, at the age of sixteen. He survived long enough to master the feat, and became the only person in the country who could make a living doing it.

Bruises, blows, burns, and lacerations were all part of rodeo competition, just as they were in the daily life of a cowboy.

Horses tumbled during races and steers thrashed while being roped. Men stumbled off the field battered and bleeding from the nose, mouth, even the ears, or lost consciousness from whiplash. One autopsy of a dead bronco rider found the man's liver had been torn loose.

But bulldogging was extreme even for rodeo. In front of the Frontier Days grandstand, Pickett leapt from a horse and grabbed a wild-eyed steer by the horns. Using his whole body for leverage, he twisted the steer's head until its nose pointed straight into the air. The thousand-pound animal bellowed and gasped for breath, its tongue dangling. The steer jerked Pickett off his feet again and again, but he held on.

Then Pickett leaned over the steer's neck and dug his teeth into the animal's lower lip. With a showman's flair he let go of the horns, threw his arms wide, and slowly sank onto his back. The steer's neck twisted even farther around, and in a moment it lost its footing and rolled over on top of him.

The crowd was dumbstruck. First-time spectators thought Pickett had surely been crushed to death. But a second later the steer rolled to the side and Pickett stood up unhurt, bowing and smiling to deafening applause.

The animal had barely staggered to its feet when Pickett did it all over again. One witness called the performance "one of the most startling and sensational exhibitions ever seen at a place where daring and thrilling feats are commonplace."

BY 1907, FRONTIER DAYS was hands down the greatest show of its kind, attracting 20,000 people to Cheyenne every summer. It was also a huge source of local pride, since Wyoming cowboys had never lost the two most prestigious events: steer roping and bronco busting. New challengers from Colorado, Arizona, and beyond only intensified the competition. "Wyoming punchers naturally wish to keep the championships in this state," wrote the *Denver Post*, "and the talent from the outside is equally determined to capture the trophies."

Frontier Days was big enough that even nonhuman performers were becoming celebrities. One infamous icon was a bronco named Steamboat, a coal-black gelding with three white feet and a white star on his forehead. He was so full of dynamite that he broke a bone in his nose while being branded (or castrated, depending on the story), leaving him with a distinctive whistling breath and a nickname that stuck.

Steamboat's reign started at Denver's Festival of Mountain and Plain in 1901 and lasted nearly a decade. In his prime, he was the most notorious bucking horse in the West, and perhaps in the country, drawing people from hundreds of miles away to watch him in action. He was a big animal, over 1,100 pounds, with the "muscles of a plow horse, but the speed of a Greyhound," as one reporter put it.

Steamboat would often squat as he was being saddled for a ride. Then:

By the time the bronc buster was set in the stirrups Steamboat's belly'd be almost touchin' the arena dust. Then, the second they'd jerk that blindfold he'd explode! He'd bust out to the middle of the arena as if he wanted the stage all to himself and he'd put on the

damnedest exhibition of sunfishing and windmilling
I ever seen. His best trick was to swap ends between
jumps and come down ker-slam on four ramrod legs.

Steamboat's signature move was a twisting kick that sent
his head and forelegs in one direction and his rump and hind
legs in another, mane and tail whipping in every direction. Almost every man who dared to mount Steamboat called him the
worst horse he ever rode. One rider said he couldn't eat anything for several days afterward. Another, who stayed on for
ten seconds, woke up lying on a blanket behind the stands with
no memory of anything beyond the first few jumps. He couldn't
speak above a whisper for a month.

"There was a portion of ham in Steamboat and a lot of
sportsmanship," one expert wrote. He never refused to buck or
bucked into a crowd, and he never kicked or trampled a rider
after throwing him. He simply "unloaded a bronco rider a day
just like clockwork and when led back by the grand stand was
applauded for his effort."

At the 1907 bucking event in Cheyenne, heavy rains had
turned the grounds into clinging mud. Eben Low was among
the crowd that day, watching Steamboat chuck rider after rider.
By the end of the competition, just two men remained: Clayton
Danks, the cowboy who had dazzled Teddy Roosevelt a few
years earlier, and a rider named John Dodge.

Dodge rode Steamboat, who bucked a hundred yards down
the field, turned around, and bucked all the way back before
launching the cowboy off his back. Dodge hit the ground so
hard he lay still for several moments before climbing to his feet.

Danks rode his bronco to a standstill and won the championship. Audiences would have to wait another year to see the superstar cowboy ride the "far-famed outlaw cayuse."

In addition to seeing a legendary bronco in top form, Eben also witnessed an outstanding steer-roping contest. While bronco riding was a battle of strength and will, roping was a test of technique and speed, and fans reacted accordingly. As one reporter put it: "The winner of a cattle-roping contest is a bronzed hero" and "an object of admiring envy to every man."

Roping also had its fair share of risk. At major rodeos like Frontier Days, steers were selected for age and bad temperament. "A 3-year-old steer is just in the prime of life as far as ability to run is concerned," explained the *Denver Times*, "and his general cussedness rises above par at that age." Their horns were fully grown as well. Thrashing steers could kick, headbutt, or gore cowboys trying to tie them up. A lassoed steer could even yank a contestant's saddle right off his horse and dash away with it.

The world roping record had been set at Frontier Days in 1906 by a cowboy named Charles "C.B." Irwin, who clocked the seemingly unbeatable time of 38.2 seconds. If any challenger in 1907 could top that, it was Wyoming's own Angus MacPhee. Thirty-two-year-old MacPhee had grown up in Chugwater, a speck of a town forty-five miles north of Cheyenne. His parents had immigrated from the Scottish island of Islay and had held on to at least a piece of their heritage; in 1886, his father founded the Islay Post Office near Laramie.

MacPhee was a slender man with a narrow nose and gray eyes. By eighteen, he was working as a bronco buster for Buffalo

Bill's Wild West in Chicago. His next job was running sup-
plies to gold miners in Alaska by dogsled. In 1898, MacPhee
joined other experienced cowboys, miners, and athletes training as part of the volunteer regiment that would come to be
known as the Rough Riders, led by Colonel Leonard Wood and
his second-in-command, Teddy Roosevelt. MacPhee and other
Cheyenne cowboys went to war in Cuba and the Philippines,
and years later, MacPhee's daughter would recall how her father and "Colonel Teddy," now president, reunited at Frontier
Days in 1903 "like two hugging bears."

MacPhee began entering rodeo contests and winning, eventually becoming a five-time Frontier Days champion. In 1907,
Eben watched closely as the Wyoming cowboy tied his first
steer in 37.4 seconds, a full second faster than Irwin's record.
Nobody else came close that round or the next. MacPhee made
another perfect throw in the finals, with a time of 58.8 seconds,
and his combined time earned him the title.

Taking in the competition from the stands, Eben was impressed by MacPhee's performance. Yet the one-handed cowboy also felt Waimea Boys like Ikua were as good as any of the
competitors gathered in Cheyenne. He had such confidence in
his fellow paniolo that he would, without hesitation, "pit them
against the finest in the world and wager my silver spurs and
$2,000 saddle against anyone in a contest with them, whether
on mountains or plains."

Even if he was wrong, a contest pitting Wyoming's best
against Hawaii's best would be worth the price of admission.
Before the results of the 1907 Frontier Days contest were even
announced, Eben decided to invite the steer-roping champion

to compete in Honolulu. He contacted the local papers and promised to cover the expenses of any cowboy who came to Hawaii for the matchup—and guaranteed him a "a royal good time."

Eben made his offer the same afternoon MacPhee was crowned Frontier Days titleholder, and the Wyoming cowboy accepted the invitation on the spot.

11

GO FETCH YOUR GLORY

EBEN LEFT FOR HAWAII aboard the steamship *Manchuria* out of San Francisco, his entrepreneurial instinct in overdrive. As one Parker Ranch cowboy put it, "God put Eben here to promote the paniolo." His experience in Cheyenne had inspired him to put together a huge rodeo and cowboy carnival in the islands.

Eben arrived in Honolulu at the end of October, picked early December as the date for a Wild West show, and got to work assembling a program. His visit to Frontier Days had shown him how important media coverage was, and he played the local papers like a pro. Eben made sure reporters knew that cowboys were coming all the way from Wyoming to compete, including world champion roper Angus MacPhee, "terror of the steers."

With Eben's prodding, the press covered MacPhee like an international celebrity and painted the contest as a show-down between the mainland champ and hometown hero Ikua Purdy. "Eben Low Says Natives Can Not Be Beaten," read one headline, followed by Eben's assertion that Texas cowboys "have nothing on the native product." The paniolo worked in tougher conditions, were better with the lasso, and—lest anyone forget—herded cows into the ocean.

Part of the promotion involved educating Hawaiian readers about the paniolo temperament, or a glamorized version of it. They were "modest, unassuming fellows, who do their work as they find it and think nothing of the performance," wrote the *Pacific Commercial Advertiser.* "Danger is their daily portion and hardship their lot, yet they are always on hand with the goods and come bad luck or good, figure it is all to be in the game . . . In this respect they certainly differ from a type of the western cowboy, with the loud mouth and the large obtrusive gun."

In many ways, Ikua did fit this image of the modest cowboy. He was quiet, relished his work, and appreciated the rhythm and independence of it. Still, before the contest in Honolulu, Ikua said he could go toe-to-toe with MacPhee—give him "a hard tussle," as he put it. After all, Ikua's top time (38.75 seconds) was barely a second slower than the Wyoming cowboy's best (37.4 seconds).

It's impossible, though, to know how much Ikua, or MacPhee for that matter, bought into Eben's narrative of epic rivalry. Ikua certainly had other things on his mind: earlier that year, his wife had delivered a stillborn child. Compared with the heartbreak of such an event, the excitement of a sporting match may not have even registered.

Nevertheless, the contest generated plenty of headline-worthy drama—hometown underdog squares off against haole champ—with an obvious subtext of colonial tension. The time had come for Hawaii's paniolo to show the mainlanders what they could do.

———

THE WILD WEST SHOW kicked off at Kapiʻolani Park on December 13, 1907. The grandstands and bleachers were nearly full, and even Queen Liliʻuokalani was there to take in the spectacle. Although she had been deposed nearly a decade prior, the people adored her. She was still their queen, and her attendance added to the pageantry of the day.

Despite heavy rains, Johnny "Cheyenne" Winters, another cowboy from Wyoming, gave a dazzling exhibition of trick roping. But when Winters went to compete, he ended up pinned beneath a horse and had to wait until the animal was lifted off his leg before he could limp from the arena. Another rider was knocked unconscious.

The action attracted a rowdy scene around the park. When dozens of Hawaiians started climbing the fences by the cattle corral, police officers used whips to push them back. A mob began shouting and taunting the mostly white officers. Someone drew a gun, but Eben intervened and managed to convince the police to back off.

More worrisome was the fact that the weather had delayed MacPhee's ship until the last possible moment. Eben had to pick the cowboy and his family up at the port and drive them to the grounds himself. The audience welcomed MacPhee with three rowdy cheers, as if he was one of their own.

When the "puncher from Wyoming" did finally mount up, he was not in peak condition; according to one account he "showed the effect of his very recent steamer experience and the heave was still in his legs and head." MacPhee missed his first pass at the steer, although his riding showed "that he is undoubtedly in a class by himself, while his quick recovery of his lariat after his first throw showed his expertness with the rope."

On MacPhee's second attempt, the crowd got a glimpse of brilliance when he caught and threw his steer in just 18 seconds. As he dismounted to make the tie, however, his horse let the rope slack and the steer regained its footing, enveloping itself and MacPhee in a cloud of dust.

MacPhee's wife, Della, and his daughter Inez were seated next to the queen. When the dust parted to reveal MacPhee pinned beneath the steer, Inez heard the crowd emit "a great sound like a wailing moan." But the young girl assured the queen that her father was fine. "He just bulldogged the steer, that's all," she said. "Papa is too smart to get hurt in a show."

A moment later, MacPhee was up, unhurt and bowing to great applause. He had lost the contest but won the crowd. (He had also gained an appreciation for island cattle: "The Hawaiian steer is a tough customer," he said later, because even when thrown they "bounce up again like a rubber ball.")

Ikua took first place in the "mavericking" contest, in which a group of cowboys pursued dozens of calves and raced to be the first to rope one, throw it to the ground, and go through the motions of branding.

The fastest calf-roping time of the day was 1:02, by a young paniolo named Makai Keliʻilike from the island of Kahoolawe. Ikua made a spectacularly fast throw, and even though his steer staggered to its feet like MacPhee's had, he was able to make the tie in 1:28—not enough to win, but hardly a disappointing performance.

The paniolo had done themselves and the islands proud. As rodeo fever spread through Hawaii, everyone wondered who was truly the best. In Waimea, Ikua and the other Parker Ranch boys practiced in Under-a-Minute corral, named for the quick times that local ropers clocked. By now Ikua was famous throughout the islands, but he was no outlier. George Lindsay, another Parker Ranch roper, tied a steer in 39.4 seconds, less than a second behind Ikua's record. At a rodeo in Hilo in February 1908, Keli'ilike won the roping contest with a time of 1 minute 6 seconds, while Archie Ka'au'a came in third. Ikua wasn't there, but Eben was, and he delighted the crowd with a roping time of 1 minute 12 seconds, which as far as anyone could tell was a record for one-armed ropers.

Also on hand in Hilo was Angus MacPhee. It had been two months since he and his family had left the mainland during a brutal Front Range blizzard and arrived in the welcoming climate of Hawaii. They decided to stay for good. At the Hilo rodeo, MacPhee failed to place in the roping contest once again, but this time a lethargic mount was to blame. According to Eben: "One of the girls up there told him that next time he had better ride the steer and rope the horse." MacPhee did win the barrel-racing competition, at least.

His streak of bad luck finally ended at a rodeo on Oahu in July 1908. On the first day, he clocked the fastest time of 1 minute 10 seconds. But the next day, Archie Ka'au'a, who had also won the half-mile pony race, managed a 55-second tie, putting

him ahead of MacPhee. The paniolo were consistently match-
ing or outperforming the Wyoming champion. But this was all
taking place in the islands, far out of sight of mainland newspapers and rodeo-goers.

BACK IN CHEYENNE, AS winter gave way to spring, Frontier Days officials were getting ready to welcome contestants from abroad.
The show had started drawing the interest of top cowboys
from places as far as Brazil and Argentina, each with their own
distinct cowboy traditions. Word of Hawaii's paniolo was fil-
tering out thanks to the recent rodeos, Eben's publicity efforts,
and Buffalo Bill Cody and his international cast of performers.
Even though the islands were now officially part of the United
States, to most Americans they might as well have been another
country.

In June 1908, Frontier Days Secretary E. W. Stone wrote
to Eben with a proposition. The rodeo's organizers would pay
travel expenses and provide room and board for a few of Eben's
best riders and ropers to compete in Cheyenne in August. All
they had to bring was their own ropes and saddles; horses
would be provided. "We will do our best to give the boys a
good time, and assure them fair treatment in all contests,"
Stone wrote. He added that Eben should send along photographs of the lads for advertising materials.

Of course Eben said yes. Steer roping was the event Hawaiians had the best chance of winning, and Ikua and Archie were
the two obvious choices. Eben later added his brother Jack to
join them. Eben himself was too busy with his various busi-

ness interests to go, but he solicited donations from other is-land ranches to ensure the three paniolo had enough money to make it all the way to Wyoming.

Ikua, Archie, and Jack had never been outside of the islands. Suddenly they were offered a free trip across the Pacific and the chance to take home some prize money. Their descendants would later say the men were thrilled at the opportunity to compete. Yet as their journey neared, they were probably ap-prehensive, too. Wyoming was synonymous with rodeo cham-pions.

The paniolo were also inadvertent emissaries. On the heels of annexation, Hawaiian cultural identity was under threat, and the islands' future under U.S. rule was uncertain. When the paniolo sailed out of Honolulu aboard the steamship *Ala-meda* on August 5, 1908, the Waimea Boys brought with them much more than saddles and lariats. They carried the hope and pride of the islands.

It was a moment that went well beyond rodeo. "We have no doubts," declared one newspaper editorial, "that these Ha-waiians will return adorned in victory in the various contests, being that it is clear that the little ability of the haole cannot match that of the Hawaiian boys in this skill . . . O Hawaiians, go fetch your glory!"

PART III

SEE AMERICA FIRST

THE SAN FRANCISCO THAT greeted the Hawaiians was practically brand new.

Two years earlier, at dawn on Wednesday, April 18, 1906, a massive earthquake ruptured 296 miles of the San Andreas Fault. The shaking, and the four days of fires that followed, killed 3,000 people and leveled four-fifths of the city. Insurance claims filed in the aftermath equaled the entire federal budget.

The rebuilding efforts involved razing entire redwood forests and working thousands of horses to death. But with stunning speed, a modern metropolis supplanted what had been a creaky Victorian port city. In three years, 20,000 new buildings rose from the ruins. Two months before the paniolo arrived, authorities had shuttered the last refugee camp set up for people who had been left homeless by the disaster.

For the country at large, the devastating earthquake did little to quash a pervasive spirit of optimism about a better future. The United States had emerged from the Spanish-American War as a confident world power. Americans in the new century didn't merely get by; they *did* things: drove automobiles, watched movies, chatted on the telephone. Every week seemed to bring new breakthroughs: skyscrapers soaring higher in Manhattan, the Wright Brothers flying farther in North Carolina, engineers digging farther across the Panama Canal.

Of course, this buoyant script was being written mostly by white men. So it's little surprise that *The San Francisco Call* noted the arrival of the "chocolate-colored rope throwers" from Hawaii. These "Kanaka cowboys," the paper said, "think they can show the product of the wild west a few things about roping steers."

Jack Low's wife, Emily, accompanied the three paniolo on their journey. Emily had dark eyes and a kind smile, and always seemed to have a book in her hand. They had been married three years before, and the trip to Wyoming was like a delayed honeymoon, an opportunity for the young couple to see the world.

When a reporter interviewed the men, Ikua, who was most comfortable speaking Hawaiian or pidgin, had little to say about the upcoming contest. Archie, however, spoke "with the simple modesty of a leading lady who knows herself a headliner and wants the world to share her knowledge." He boasted of winning the island championship: "I roped, threw and tied four steers in 1 minute and 35 seconds."

"And Mr. Purdy, is he a champion, also?" asked the reporter.

"Purdy? Well, I believe Purdy did the trick once in 38 3/4 seconds. But it was only one steer. My time was for four steers." Whether Archie said this with an elbow and a wink to his cousin, the reporter didn't say.

———

THE NEXT MORNING THE Hawaiians traveled to the Ferry Building on the Embarcadero for the first step of their overland journey to Cheyenne. They had never seen a structure like it. Each of the clock faces on the 245-foot tower was the size of a small corral. Crowds surged under its long arched arcades. Inside the building, sunbeams fell through the skylights that ran the length of the Great Nave, two stories high and longer than two football fields.

Eyes wide, the paniolo made their way through the multitudes and boarded a ferry across San Francisco Bay, a fresh west wind pushing away the morning fog.

As the ferry drew closer to Oakland, the passengers could see a forest of ships' masts lining the Central Pacific Railroad's two-mile Long Wharf, where freight trains waited to load and unload cargo. The paniolo found the Southern Pacific's No. 2 Overland Limited waiting at the Oakland pier.

Operating the western half of a route that ran from San Francisco to Chicago, the Overland was the finest rail experience in the West, and possibly the country. The train had electric lights, drawing rooms, and smoking parlors. The Hawaiians could eat in the buffet car or the ritzier dining car, with food and service comparable to the most upscale restaurant. They moved between cars thanks to the recently invented closed vestibule, and took in the scenery from the open rear platform of the observation car. Emily would have been at home in the library car, stocked with carefully curated volumes of fiction

and travel. Jack might not have loved the engine smoke coming
in through the open windows, aggravating his asthma.

To a cowboy from Hawaii—or the average mainlander,
for that matter—the Overland Limited was like a luxury hotel
speeding along at thirty miles an hour. But what made it truly
exceptional wasn't the brass fixtures in the washrooms or the
starched sheets in the pull-down Pullman beds. It was the route
itself, a sweeping introduction to the landscapes and history of
the American West. Much of the Overland's itinerary traced in
reverse the paths of explorers and wagon trains that had ventured toward the Pacific just decades before.

After a mid-morning departure, the Overland left the smelt-
ing works, sugar refineries, and waterfront canneries of Oakland. It passed the town of Rodeo, whose name recalled the
days of Spanish vaqueros and their annual roundups. The train
was then divided into segments and rolled aboard the paddle
steamer *Solano*, then the largest ferryboat in the world, for a
short hop across a branch of San Pablo Bay.

The Overland continued into the broad, fertile Sacramento
Valley, where workers from Mexico and East Asia tended crops.
It was open country, dotted with groves of spreading oaks
whose twisted branches recalled the koa trees on the slopes of
Mauna Kea.

Gold-dusted Sacramento came next. In addition to being
the nexus of the 1849 California gold rush, the state capital was
home to a colony of about a hundred native Hawaiians who had
been brought by pioneer John Sutter to work at Sutter's Fort.[*]

---

[*] Sutter also owned the mill where gold was discovered in 1848.

The Hawaiians settled at the junction of the Feather and Sacramento Rivers. *The San Francisco Call* described how the "big
brown men and women" held luau, danced hula, and intermar-
ried with members of the local Maidu tribe. ("The salubrious
climate," the writer noted, "is engendering in this languorous
race an aptitude for labor.")

From Sacramento, the Overland steamed toward the peaks
of the Sierra Nevada. Orchards of pears and prunes gave way to
evergreen forests as the engine slowed and strained against the
increasing grade. The paniolo had been on higher mountains—
Mauna Kea tops out at almost 14,000 feet—but there was nothing on Hawaii like the sheer granite relief of the Sierras.

Sunset came just as the Overland crested 7,000-foot Donner
Pass, where, in the winter of 1846–1847, a snowbound party of
pioneers had had to resort to cannibalism. Two decades later,
railroad crews tackled the hardest engineering challenge on
the transcontinental route: digging and blasting seven tunnels
through solid rock, in a place where the snow could pile up to
forty feet high. No traveler could pass through these tunnels
without marveling at the monumental labor it had taken to lay
the tracks.

Ninety percent of those laborers were Chinese, brought to
the United States to fill a shortage of workers in the West. They
endured backbreaking work and institutionalized racism, living in segregated line camps like the one that came through
Cheyenne. Resentment over the fact that they worked for less
than whites led to the Chinese Exclusion Act of 1882. The only
federal legislation in American history to ban immigrants of a
specific ethnicity, it also forbade Chinese who were already in

the country from becoming citizens. The law wasn't repealed until 1943.

The August light was fading as the Overland pulled into the lumber town of Truckee. Forest fires had destroyed the city over half a dozen times already, and the paniolo and Emily likely saw the glow of yet another blaze that was burning east of town. From Truckee, passengers on the Overland sped in comfort across the merciless landscape of northern Nevada, sweltering even at night despite the breeze through the open windows.

The sun was up by the time the train entered Utah. Travelers sipped their morning coffee and watched the landscape flatten and bleach into the otherworldly Great Salt Lake Desert, where the salt flats stretched south like an infinite sheet of paper.

Just forty miles south of the rail line was the most isolated community of Hawaiians on the mainland. Iosepa, Utah, was named after the Mormon elder Joseph F. Smith, who had served as a missionary in the islands and was the nephew of the Mormon prophet Joseph Smith. Native Hawaiian converts to the Church of Jesus Christ of Latter-Day Saints had first immigrated to Salt Lake City in the 1870s, but they experienced such discrimination in the Utah capital that church leadership decided they would be "better off" living somewhere else.

That somewhere was Skull Valley, Utah, a setting as unlike Polynesia as anywhere on Earth. When the first forty-six Hawaiian settlers arrived in the valley in August 1889, they found a desolate basin hemmed in by mountains at the southwest corner of the Great Salt Lake. The islanders could handle the heat, even the dryness, but the bitter winters and economic hardship were almost too much. As the Hawaiians huddled in poorly insulated homes, their children died from whooping cough. Eventually the settlers started growing crops, raising carp in ponds, and mining gold from the nearby mountains, and by 1908 the population of Iosepa was almost 200.

But leaving Salt Lake City didn't mean the Hawaiians had left prejudice behind. When a handful of leprosy cases broke out in Iosepa, Utah papers blamed the Pacific Islanders for bringing the "devil's disease." Hawaii had a well-known leper colony on Molokai at the time, where people with advanced cases were relocated, and whites believed Hawaiians were more susceptible to the illness.*

Residents of Iosepa pined for their lost homes, painting images of whales and sea turtles on the walls of caves above the town. In 1917, six years after Iosepa won an award as "the most progressive city in Utah," the church president emptied the settlement. Even though many of the younger residents knew nothing besides life in Utah, the church ordered them all to return to Hawaii to help build a temple on Oahu. The Skull Valley land was sold and the homes and irrigation canals the settlers had struggled to build were abandoned.

As the Overland pushed east into the Wasatch Mountains, the paniolo marveled at formations such as Devil's Slide, a pair of parallel limestone ridges plunging downhill for hundreds of feet, and Pulpit Rock, the massive boulder where the Mormon

---

* At its peak, the settlement of Kalaupapa, Molokai, was home to 1,200 men, women, and children. The isolation law lasted until 1969.

prophet Brigham Young was said to have preached his first sermon in Utah. In Echo Canyon, the railroad tracks crossed and recrossed a mountain torrent under gray masses of stone. The shriek of the locomotive echoed off cliffs and peaks tinted red with iron.

Then, finally, came the arid hills and flatlands of southern Wyoming. Soon it was night again. Green River, Rawlins, Laramie, the Continental Divide—all came and went in the darkness. Less than an hour after sunrise, at 6:35 A.M. on Friday, August 14, 1908, the Overland groaned to a stop in Cheyenne and the islanders stepped down onto the platform.

WITH SIX DAYS TO go before the rodeo, Wyoming's capital was in a frenzy of preparation. The city expected up to 30,000 spectators. Every bed in town was full, from the $3.50-a-night rooms at the Inter-Ocean Hotel to the 15-cent bunks at the Salvation Workman's Hotel, coffee and doughnuts included.

North of the city, a new Frontier Park stood on what had until recently been a flat swath of prairie. A freshly scraped and rolled dirt racetrack surrounded a grassy area for bronco busting and steer roping. An eight-foot steel fence enclosed the whole park, and workers were putting the final touches on a new steel grandstand. Downtown, men were busy stringing up copper cables to power a new streetcar system, with a spur that ran straight to the park. Four plush streetcars, each big enough to hold 125 passengers, were due to arrive from Denver any day.

The city that once was "the scene of many a cowboy orgie [*sic*]", was now "highly respectable and peaceful," wrote the *Wyoming Times*. Cheyenne had endured highs and lows since its birth as a railroad outpost forty years earlier, to emerge as a cosmopolitan state capital with more than 10,000 residents. It boasted streets lined with splendid homes and bustling downtown businesses. The Atlas Theatre had recently opened a block from the train depot, with 550 seats, a large stage, a penny arcade, and a soda fountain.

In March, the first round-the-world car race had passed through en route from New York to Paris the long way, via Asia and the Pacific. The lead car, driven by an American team, was met by the "greatest public demonstration since the famous ride of president Roosevelt," and rolled down 17th Street accompanied by a band of cowboys. August brought "the largest tent ever made with the greatest circus human eyes ever beheld": the Barnum & Bailey Circus.

Even as Cheyenne followed the rest of the country in a mad hustle toward tomorrow, the Old West lived on. In the weeks leading up to the rodeo, a Wyoming policeman arrested Bert Starr, one of the West's most notorious horse thieves. The papers praised the officer's bravery, since Starr was found to be armed with two knives and three guns, and "not only has a strong aversion to officers in general, but is a dead shot." Just two days before Frontier Days opened, news of the day included a report that a twelve-year-old girl in the town of Big Muddy had killed a "monster" rattlesnake by crushing its head with a pair of iron horse hobbles.

Frontier Days depended on this wild reputation. Indeed, it cashed in on it. The "Grand Pageant of the West That Was" was a place for westerners to preserve and revel in their history—at least a white man's version of it—and share it with anyone willing to pay for the privilege. The participants, the events they competed in, the between-act entertainment, even the city itself were all just a step or two removed from the actual frontier. This aura of authenticity, *The Denver Times* wrote, was what made it unique:

> There is no professionalism about the show, save the professionalism which spends its days in the saddle, and its nights sleeping on the ground; that faces blizzards in winter and torching heat in summer; that conquers wild horses and fights wild beasts—the professionalism that made the West of today a possibility.

The country's budding domestic tourism industry had started promoting travel through the still-exotic West as "a ritual of American citizenship." The railroad companies ran publicity campaigns encouraging wealthy Americans to forgo their next European vacation and "See America First." The public was hungry to see a world it had read about in books like *The Virginian*, the first successful "western" novel, set in central Wyoming, and silent films like *The Great Train Robbery*. By 1908, many visitors to Frontier Days were "residents of the effete east," as the *Wyoming Times* put it, in search of an experience to cap off their first summer traveling beyond the Mississippi:

> From what the tenderfoot has heard and read, the great west is still peopled with grizzled men with buckskin

shirts, or hairy chaparejos, and he strains his eyes from the car windows to catch the glimpse of . . . the characters which his favorite fiction has taught him people the west. He will look in vain, for he is looking for the west as it was. The conditions that raised up the heroes of the pioneer days are rapidly passing away . . . but for one notable exception.

That exception was Frontier Days, which offered "no cheap imitations or sugarcoating to sweeten the tongues of the tenderfoot." It was the real thing, "triumphantly beckoning the world to see that courage, daring, strength and skill are still to be found even in this new and more modern west, if one but knows where to look."

The rough-knuckled honesty of the rodeo was something that could never be captured in a dime novel, a movie clip, or a magazine article. It had to be seen live.

LOCAL RANCHER, RODEO CHAMP, and owner of the notorious bronc Steamboat, C.B. Irwin greeted the paniolo and Emily at the train station. Irwin was a giant and gregarious man, a cowboy-entrepreneur with a booming voice and personality to match. Originally from Missouri, he brought his wife, son, and three daughters to Cheyenne in 1903, where they eventually adopted or fostered seventeen more children.

In 1906, Irwin had won the Frontier Days steer-roping title with a world record time of 38.2 seconds. He helped run the rodeo during its early years, while still competing as a roper and racehorse owner. His dual role as organizer and contestant opened the door for some light scheming, wrote one contemporary: "While Charlie liked the limelight, he also was inspired by the fact that if managed right he could make a few dollars for himself, a natural event, of course." Irwin entered Thoroughbreds in races that were meant for cow horses only, giving his riders a decided speed advantage.

He was a gracious host to the Hawaiians, introducing them to a friend who owned a ranch just outside town where they would be staying. Meanwhile, Cheyenne locals had been anticipating the Hawaiians' arrival for weeks. When the *Wyoming Tribune* ran their photo on its front page, the city was already full of speculation about how much of a threat the "lithe youngsters from the far Pacific" posed, if any.

The tenor of newspaper coverage of the paniolo mixed curiosity, disdain, and halfhearted respect. The Hawaiians may have been champions back home, but this was the heartland of cowboy country, not some tropical speck halfway around the world. To anyone unaware of Hawaii's status as a U.S. territory (read: most Americans), these men weren't just the first competitors from outside the continental United States. They were foreigners. It would have been radical to refer to them as American, and sheer blasphemy to point out that Hawaii's cattle culture predated Wyoming's—not that anyone knew.

Race and racism were already headline news in the summer of 1908. The same day the Hawaiians arrived in Cheyenne, a riot erupted in Springfield, Illinois, after a white woman accused a black man of sexual assault. Mobs of whites roamed Abraham Lincoln's hometown for the next three days, burning black homes and businesses and brutalizing anyone who resisted. Six people died and more than a hundred were injured.*

Yet while most of American society remained segregated and hostile toward any attempt at change, the world of sports was inching toward integration. Three weeks earlier, John Taylor, the son of former slaves, ran as part of the winning 1,600-meter relay team at the Olympic games in London. He was the first African American to win an Olympic gold medal. Charles Follis, "The Black Cyclone," had become the first professional American football player when he signed with an Ohio team in 1904, the same year Frontier Days had cheered Bill Pickett's bulldogging. In Pennsylvania, the Carlisle Indian Industrial School football team was taking on—and defeating—powerhouses like Harvard, Syracuse, and Penn.

In 1902, lightweight boxer Joe Gans had become the first African American world champion. Six years later he was joined by heavyweight Jack Johnson. Marshall "Major" Taylor, a black track cyclist, won the world 1-mile championship in Montreal in 1899. In horse racing, black jockeys won fifteen out of the first twenty-eight runnings of the Kentucky Derby. And just four years after the paniolo competed in Frontier Days, Hawaii's Duke Kahanamoku became an international sensation when he competed as a swimmer in the 1912 Olympic Games and introduced the world to the sport of surfing. Bigotry and segregation were still the norm, but athletes of color were starting to play on the same fields as white men—and winning.

---

*The woman who made the original accusation eventually recanted, saying her attacker had not in fact been black.

In Hawaii, the question of fair play for their boys in Cheyenne was an issue before the contest even started. Hawaiians
wondered, for good reason, whether the paniolo would be
cheated out of an honest shot at the title. After all, they were
malihini, outsiders, and would be dependent on their hosts for
horses as well as refereeing during the competition. Jack Low
even brought letters from Wyomingites in the islands urging
the Frontier Days organizers to give the paniolo "a very square
deal."

The Honolulu papers reported "some attempts at partial-
ity" in Cheyenne, "an evident wish on the part of the management of the show that the championship this year should not
go outside of Cheyenne." As a result, "things were made about
as hard for [the Hawaiians] as they could [be] without being
off color." The article made no specific allegations, but anyone
with experience in rodeo knew of at least one way a cowboy
could easily be hobbled in competition: through his horse.

In steer roping, perhaps more than in any other event, the
bond between man and horse is critical. Even the best roper
in the world has little chance on a badly trained or unfamiliar
mount. The event organizers had promised to supply horses
for the paniolo to use in competition, but days went by with
no sign of them. Frustrated, the cowboys had little choice but
to pass the time visiting Frontier Park each day, where they sat
on the fence and watched their opponents practice.

About two days before the rodeo started, the paniolo finally received their horses. They found the animals to be well
trained—Archie called them "fast and intelligent," but also too
hardmouthed, meaning they were accustomed to rougher han-

dling than Hawaiian cow ponies were. That could cause communication problems between man and horse, which in turn could cost precious seconds in competition. It was one more obstacle the Hawaiians had to overcome.

Other rodeos around the country claimed to crown champions, but no title carried as much weight as Frontier Days. Winning in Cheyenne made a man the undisputed world champion, the rodeo equivalent of Olympic gold. To mainlanders, the idea of a cowboy from outside the state, let alone from Polynesia, taking home top honors was laughable.

Into this world of outsize cockiness came the Hawaiians, their heavy rawhide lariats drawing quizzical looks from the cowboys who had gathered to scope out the newcomers. But when they were finally able to practice, it became clear how deadly accurate the paniolo could throw. The smirks began to fade.

13

OPENING DAY

EARLY IN THE MORNING of August 20, a band of cowboys in white and yellow silk shirts galloped through the streets of Cheyenne, followed by cowgirls in brightly colored shirtwaists, cowboy hats, and riding skirts. The assembled crowds waved their hats and howled, *"Hip hip hip, ki-yi ki-yi ki-yi, wau-o-o-o-o-o-o-o-o!"*

At high noon, the rumble of thousands of hooves shook the ground of Frontier Park, marking the opening of the festivities. Under darkening clouds, 1,500 cowboys, cowgirls, U.S. troops, and Native Americans dashed in a wide circle around the arena. "Moving-picture men" cranked their cameras.

The schedule was largely the same every day, with competitions spaced between exhibitions and lighter fare. For bronco riding and steer roping, the first two days consisted of heats to narrow down the field of competitors, followed by a final showdown on the third day. One entertainer was a sharpshooter from Nebraska named Captain A. H. Hardy, whom Eben had met the year before. Hardy was known for feats like hitting thousands of small wooden balls out of the air without missing. (His record was 13,066 in a row.) Hardy's new stunt for this year's rodeo was shooting glass balls with a .22 rifle while seated in a car that was speeding around the track.

But most spectators were there for the marquee events: bronco riding and steer roping. The horses picked for the bucking contest were advertised as "the toughest lot ever dragged into a show arena." One mount, "a regular spittin' kitten," fought so hard he had to be roped and thrown just to get a saddle on him. Clayton Danks, the previous year's champion, drew a mount named Dynamite that was known for unpredictable sunfishing and high-jumping maneuvers. But Danks rode him perfectly, sitting straight up and scraping with his spurs, and his performance earned him a place in the finals.

Another bronco rider almost didn't make it there in time to compete. Dick Stanley had climbed off the train from Portland, Oregon, an hour before the event, unpacked his saddle, pulled on a pair of chaps, and hurried to Frontier Park. Stanley, who ran a Wild West show in the Pacific Northwest, had entered the bucking contest by mail. He was described as a "dapper little fellow" who weighed barely 120 pounds soaking wet. A long goatee and fringed buckskin outfit gave him the look of a young Buffalo Bill. His ensemble drew dismissive snorts from the other competitors, who favored high-necked shirts and jeans. "That outfit's four-flushing, show-off stuff," one man said.

But the "over-dressed upstart from Oregon" was tough as saddle leather. Stanley had already paid his dues as a bronco buster: he had cracked ribs, busted knees, and broken both legs and a shoulder. He was twenty-eight, but according to the *Wyoming Times*, he looked forty.

Stanley stuck tight to a bronco named Fighting Sam, and his solid ride drew generous applause from the audience. The judges picked him and Danks to go on to the finals, setting the stage for one of the great showdowns in rodeo history.

WHEN IT WAS TIME for steer roping, the stands were buzzing with talk of the three men from across the Pacific. Everyone knew the paniolo were in town—"world beaters with a rope" one newspaper called them. But hardly any of the spectators had actually seen them in action, in part because it took so long to get them horses.

When the Hawaiians appeared at Frontier Park, the audience and other cowboys paused to take them in: ornate leather chaps, long rawhide lariats, flowers around their hats, and dark skin—they were different in every way. To locals and tourists in Cheyenne, the paniolo were not just odd; they were interlopers. The *Wyoming Times* reported that Ikua had "promised to come to Cheyenne and make good his defeat of MacPhee," last year's champion, "against all comers." Whether or not this was accurate—it sounded more like something Eben would say— to Frontier Days fans, the Hawaiians had thrown down the gauntlet.

Half the roping contestants competed the first day, half on the second, with the best to face off in the finals. The steers picked for the event were small and fast, making for harder lassoing and a more entertaining show. A smaller animal was also more likely to roll over completely and back onto its feet when a cowboy tried to throw it to the ground.

First out was a Wyoming cowboy who caught his white-faced steer on his first cast. But his horse let the rope go slack, and the steer scrambled back to its feet. A second throw caught the steer by the leg and snapped it. An agent from the Humane Society ran out and led the limping animal out of the arena and out of sight. A moment later came the sharp crack of a gun, the *Daily Leader* reported, "and the animal that was galloping three minutes before had become merely beef for the Indians."

One youngster drew whistles when he nailed his steer on his first cast and tied it in 33.8 seconds. This would have beaten the world record by three seconds, if only the steer hadn't struggled free. Other ropers failed to finish within the three-minute cutoff and were disqualified.

Jack Low was the only Hawaiian scheduled to rope on the first day. When his turn came, the stands fells silent. No more speculation about the Hawaiians; now it was time to see them ride. Roping on flat grass was a world away from the rocky slopes of Mauna Kea. Jack knew that, just as he knew every steer was unpredictable. He gripped the reins tightly and waited.

The steer sprinted straight down the field, with Jack close behind on his new and unfamiliar horse.

In the West, a cowboy roped with the near end of his lasso tied to his saddle horn. The simple act of stopping the horse pulled the rope taut and brought the animal down.

But paniolo operated in terrain where having a running steer attached to your saddle was a bad idea. If things went sideways—if an animal fell off a cliff or into a hidden lava tube, if the rope got tangled in the trees—the forces involved could be deadly, as Eben Low could attest. Instead, a Hawaiian often threw his loop with the other end held freely in the opposite hand. He could tie it one-handed around the saddle horn if the throw looked good, but he could also let go in a split second if he had to. The technique wasn't foolproof, but it was safer. In competition, though, it meant an extra step and extra time.

Jack hurled his loop, caught the steer by one forefoot, and dallied quickly. The steer slammed to the ground and he dismounted to make the tie. But his horse let the rope fall slack, and the steer clambered to its feet. Jack had to throw the steer to the ground twice more to pin it. By the time he was ready to make the tie, his lungs felt like they were being bound up themselves: the dust and exertion had triggered an asthma attack.

Gasping for air, Jack finally looped the piggin' string around the steer's feet and stepped back. His time: 2 minutes 25 seconds. It was an unimpressive debut for the islanders. Anyone who had doubts the Hawaiians were in the same league as mainland cowboys was feeling smug.

Next up was Pete Dickerson, a tall, stout cowboy with blue eyes and a slight limp. Dickerson had worked his way across Arizona and New Mexico as a stockman, freighter, and deputy sheriff. A favorite to win at Frontier Days in 1907, he made such a miserable showing that he vowed to stay in Cheyenne, train, and redeem himself the following year. The papers even called him "America's hope." But he was a different kind of rival from MacPhee, now comfortable in his new home in Hawaii. Dickerson was a genuine villain: just two weeks before the matchup against the paniolo, he had sexually assaulted his schoolteacher neighbor.

With his first cast, Dickerson just missed the steer. But his second throw hit home, and the animal flipped violently in midair. Dickerson finished tying in 1 minute 11 seconds, the best time of the day.

THAT EVENING A MERRY mass of humanity packed the streets and sidewalks of Cheyenne. The air was filled with catcalls and cowboy yells, and strings of red, white, and blue lights shone like stars.

Visitors who succumbed to the temptation to try to dress like a cowboy could buy a silk shirt for $5. ("Cowhands could have more pleasure out of five dollars in many ways," one real cowboy grumbled.) The "dude cowpoke" look didn't work for everyone, reported one paper: "Generally the effect of the resulting combination of extremes in styles is incongruous almost to grotesqueness and the victim of the delusion that a shirt and a hat make a westerner becomes a target for jibes."

For entertainment, there was Dyer's Hotel and Bar, "a place where a gentleman gets a gentleman's drink," or the Atlas Theatre, showing the latest moving pictures from Edison Studios and the French studio Pathé Frères. Mischief-makers of all ages used feather-ended ticklers, tin noisemakers, and "sparking electric sticks" to amuse and annoy.

Visitors who made their way to a mammoth tent at 24th and Bent Streets found it packed with people gazing upward. On top of a forty-foot tower, a girl in a red dress sat bareback astride a horse. Below them was a tank of water nine feet deep. After the announcer had whipped up the crowd for the "Fugacious Frolic with Fate" it was about to witness, the horse and girl leapt into the air.

In the days leading up to the rodeo, the Cheyenne papers were filled with full-page ads for the Great Carver Diving Horse Combination, promising "The Niagara of Sensations, Whirlpool of Realism, A Fascinating, Fearful, Flirting Incarnation of Ingenuity." F. W. Carver, a dentist, exhibition shooter, and former partner of Buffalo Bill's, had come up with a zinger of an act: a young woman diving into a water tank on horseback. Carver's daughter Lorena became famous for performing the trick as "The Girl in Red," and insisted that trained horses were often so eager to jump that it was hard to hold them back.

Every night during Frontier Days, Carver stood before the packed house and offered $100 in gold to anyone who would take the plunge and stay on the horse until it surfaced. No one ever did. Then Lorena rode her father's horse Silver King to the edge of the tower platform and into space. Girl and horse landed in an explosion of water. After five seconds of breathless silence, the horse's muzzle broke the surface, followed by Lorena. She rode the horse up a ramp and out of the tank, looking, as one paper reported, "a picture of fairyland."*

If the Hawaiians were out and about during that evening in Cheyenne, they kept to themselves. Meanwhile, at the theater performances and cowboy dances, inside saloons and

---

*By the 1930s the show had moved to Atlantic City's Steel Pier, where its new performer was Harriet Keonaonalaulani Purdy Kauaihilo, Ikua's niece, billed as the "Hawaiian Human Cannonball."

boardinghouses, on front porches and boardwalks, people were comparing impressions of the day's events, especially the showing by the first island cowboy. Maybe all that fuss about the Hawaiian riders had been for nothing.

ON DAY TWO, THE stands and bleachers of Frontier Park were filled to capacity. Cars, carriages, and riders on horseback crowded against the fence around the track. Ikua and Archie were scheduled to rope, and nobody wanted to miss seeing if the Hawaiian champion could live up to his billing.

The rodeo started at one P.M. under a cloudless sky. Marie Danks, Clayton's wife, won the ladies' relay race, even though the audience clearly backed Lillie Nicholson of Colorado. Nicholson received an ovation for her second-place finish. As *The Denver Post* put it, "When a young lady is gritty, as well as pretty, she wins the crowd."

The wolf-roping event was advertised as a fun free-for-all at the expense of one of the most feared and hated animals in the West. But watching cowboys chase down two terrified, half-grown canines didn't go over well. One young wolf immediately tried to hide in the grass, trembling, until it was "nearly smothered under a cloud of ropes." The other wolf made it fifty yards before being lassoed and dragged down the field behind a galloping horse. One paper noted that "the crowd's resentment of this barbarous and unexpected cruelty was instantaneous." Wolf roping never appeared on the schedule again.

Every day of Frontier Days, hundreds of agitated animals had to be led between the arena and corrals. Every so often a horse or steer escaped and ran amok. If it ended up in the tightly packed crowd, someone could be hurt badly, or worse. During the second day of the 1908 competition, two horses broke loose. The first was headed straight for the stands when the loop of a lasso settled around its neck, bringing it to a quick halt. Holding the other end was Archie Kaʻauʻa.

The second runaway was also caught by a paniolo. Ikua made a difficult throw from horseback. There was another horse between him and the fugitive, so he had to throw his lariat up and over the other animal. The loop landed "just in time to drop the festival trouble-maker in his tracks." It wasn't technically part of the rodeo, but anyone who saw the scene and knew a thing or two about cowboy craft had to have been impressed.

Finally it was time for steer roping. Jack may have been the first paniolo to compete, but Ikua and Archie were the ones with the winning records. It was time for the "dusky wizards of the rawhide" to prove their mastery.

There were eight other contestants on the roster for the second day of competition; the best two would compete tomorrow against Dickerson and Clark, the first day's winners.

Half a dozen locals went first. C.B. Irwin made a textbook bust, and when he sprang up from making the tie, the clock read 58 seconds. The crowd whooped and hollered, thinking the Hawaiians had been beat before they even began. But just then, the steer slipped one foot loose. Time ran out before Irwin could retie the animal, and he was out of the competition. The next three contestants also failed to complete their ties.

Archie rode into position under a sky darkening with clouds. Dickerson's 1 minute 11 seconds remained the time to beat.

Archie's steer took a flying start. The red flag flashed, and Archie spurred his white horse forward, whirling his lasso overhead.

He closed in on the steer at full speed and snapped his loop over the animal's head. But unlike the other ropers, he waited until the rope worked its way to the steer's midsection before cinching it with a tug.

The steer kept running, and the loop slipped over its narrow hips and down its back legs. When the rope reached its heels, Archie made another quick jerk and the loop tightened. This was a classic paniolo move: a solid heel catch was safer than roping an animal by the horns. It laid a steer out, knocking the wind out of it, but rarely caused injury.

A moment later, though, the downed steer twisted to its feet and bolted for the low fence bordering the racetrack. Archie tried to run his horse around the animal, but it kept dodging in the same direction, twice, then three times. He threw again just as the steer tried to leap over the fence, catching it straight on the heels this time.

The steer was in midair as Archie dallied, then reined in his horse so hard it heaved back on its haunches.

The rope snapped tight and the steer turned a complete somersault, landing half over the fence with its head off the ground. Archie was on it instantly to make the tie.

It was a fantastic bust. When Archie's time was announced— 1 minute 9 seconds, the fastest yet—the grandstand burst into applause.

Two other competitors followed Archie, but their times didn't even come close.

Then it was Ikua's turn. He wore a striped sweater and tight white breeches. Twenty thousand pairs of eyes watched as the famous Hawaiian cowboy rode out on a huge buckskin gelding.

Ikua's steer took off so quickly he didn't have a chance to throw until they had both sprinted more than halfway down the field. Worse, he found his horse wouldn't respond instantly to the reins. So Ikua made a fast side throw, opening a loop big enough for the steer to run through.

He took one turn of rope around the saddle horn to slow its run. The loop cinched around the steer's midsection and a cry went up from the audience. Roping an animal by the feet, as Jack and Archie had, was strange enough. But lassoing a steer around the waist was lunacy.

"That settles HIM," a man in the press box said. "He'll never bust that steer in a thousand years."

But the spectators didn't know how many times Ikua had made exactly that kind of throw on the slopes of Mauna Kea. His horse darted around the steer, and when the loop was around its hind feet, Ikua finished his dally. The rawhide twanged like a harp string and the steer hit the ground with a noise that carried to the back row of the grandstand.

Ikua leapt off his horse and bent over the stunned animal. He would later say of the crowd: "I could not hear myself tie up the steer." He finished the tie and jumped to his feet with his hands in the air. There was a breathless moment before the judges announced his time: 1 minute 3 seconds. Frontier Park erupted.

Fans had gotten their money's worth, and there was still one more day to go.

14

A LESSON IN HOW
TO HANDLE STEERS

HAT NIGHT, RAIN AND mud drove visitors indoors. One cowboy ball had a full orchestra, but instead of a symphony it performed "the good breezy ragtime, two step and quadrilles full of ginger the cowboy loves." The papers assured visitors that "the cowboys, though dressed after the manner of the range, are all gentlemen, and some of them fancy dancers," and that any ladies who attended would "be guaranteed the utmost courtesy and a real good time."

Emily and the paniolo drew lots of attention, but they weren't the only Pacific Islanders in Cheyenne. That night, lilting Hawaiian melodies and the twang of steel guitar filled the Atlas Theatre when the groundbreaking musical trio of July, "Toots" Paka, and Joseph Kekuku took the stage. The baritone singer and guitarist Iolai ("July") Kealoha Paka was a favorite of Queen Lili'uokalani. He traveled to San Francisco to launch his career, and eventually made one of the first known recordings of Hawaiian music.

July married Hannah Jones, a Broadway actress from Michigan who reinvented herself as "Toots" Paka. The couple toured vaudeville theaters across the country, with July playing guitar and singing and Toots performing the hula, dressed as a South Seas princess. (Even though she had studied hula in the islands, Hawaiians weren't always won over; one critic called her performance "as piquant as a picnic in the rain.") The trio was completed by guitarist Joseph Kekuku. As a boy, Kekuku laid a guitar flat in his lap and experimented sliding a metal bar up and down the strings. In doing so, he invented the swooping sound of Hawaiian steel guitar.

Together, Kekuku and the Pakas were the first supergroup of Hawaiian music, eventually playing some of the largest venues in the country. In Cheyenne, the paniolo may have attended the show—there's no record either way—but it's hard to imagine they were unaware the musicians were in town.

Meanwhile, some evening celebrations took on a rougher edge. A drunk and belligerent cowboy had to be ejected from a theater; a visitor from Kansas who had also tipped back a few too many fell through the plate glass window of a pharmacy; downtown, a quarreling couple "found their quarters too small for free action and went into the street to settle their domestic difficulties in primitive tooth and nail fashion."

Local cowboys had good reason to hit the bottle: their world had just been shaken. "Hawaiians Beat Westerners Roping Steers," blared one headline—"They Are Dangerously Quick." Another account described Ikua's performance as "one of the prettiest busts of the tournament." As the *Daily Leader* put it, the Hawaiians had "invaded the heart of the American cow country and taught the white ropers a lesson in how to handle steers." At least one bartender had had enough. When Ikua and the others ordered drinks in his saloon, he refused to serve them.

NOT EVEN TERRIBLE WEATHER could demoralize rodeo-goers on the third and final day. A cold drizzle "chilled the bleacherites to the bone and sent the umbrellas up like hundreds of black mushrooms." Fans had come to see champions crowned, and they were staying.

Five men had made it to the bronco-busting finals, including Clayton Danks and Dick Stanley. Stanley had a strong first ride. The next three competitors all failed to impress the judges, and then it was Danks's turn. The defending champion's horse had drawn as many spectators as any of the riders: Steamboat.

Danks and Steamboat had met at Frontier Days the previous year. "There are other outlaws that do more fancy steps when they're bucking," the cowboy said, "but they don't jar a man like Steamboat . . . he gives sort of peculiar, side twisting jumps, and when he hits the ground you think you've fell off one of those twenty-story teepees." That year both had come away winners: Danks was crowned world champion bronco rider, and Steamboat was awarded worst bucking horse.

This particular day Danks stayed on the infamous bronco, but he didn't use his spurs, which made for a comparatively bland ride. Spectators wondered if Steamboat's best days were behind him; after all, the horse was fourteen years old. But old hands in the audience knew that no man had ever spurred Steamboat and ridden him to a finish.

The judges decided that Stanley and Danks would have a one-on-one final matchup to determine the winner. Stanley hadn't expected to make it to the finals at all and had already taken a considerable beating. Now he was just one ride away from the title.

Cold wet wind swept across the arena as Stanley brushed off his purple shirt and climbed into the saddle. The second the blindfold was pulled off, Stanley raised his right boot and raked his spurs down Steamboat's flank.

The horse went mad with fury. He whirled and plunged, leaping straight up and landing with a crash. Horse and rider zigzagged across the field and jumped the fence onto the track, which had been churned into deep mud by the day's races. Stanley's right foot kept moving up and down like a piston.

The crowd realized what was happening and broke into a roar, chanting "Stanley! Stanley! Stanley!" The furious animal gradually slowed and then stopped. Stanley, battered but smiling, waved his free arm overhead. Steamboat gave one final surprise leap sideways, but the Oregon cowboy stayed on, still spurring as the horse came to a standstill once more.

It was over. An assistant caught the horse's head and Stanley dismounted, stumbled a few steps, and fell into the waiting arms of supporters. He had done the impossible: spur Steamboat and survive. In the words of one reporter, it was "the greatest and the gamest exhibition" of bronco riding that Cheyenne, if not the world, had ever seen.

Danks, a Frontier Days legend, delivered a technically flawless but uninspiring ride, and Stanley seemed like the clear winner. Yet the judges, inexplicably, wouldn't declare a champion. There were grumbles of hometown bias. When it was announced the men would have to ride once more, the air filled with hisses and howls of objection.

Stanley somehow mustered the energy to mount up one more time. He and Danks each rode new horses, spurring throughout. When it was over, Stanley was barely able to walk, but Danks was there to offer his rival a hand. "Old man," he said, "you're the toughest proposition I ever rode against. Shake."

Inexplicably, it took the judges another three hours to reach a decision: Stanley was the champion. He was the first cowboy from outside Wyoming to win the Frontier Days bucking title—but when it was time to claim his prize, he was nowhere to been seen.

AS IF ON CUE, the sun came out just in time for the steer-roping finals. Umbrellas were folded and dripping hats shaken dry. The stands were buzzing. Two impossible things had just happened: Steamboat had been spurred to a standstill, and an outsider had won the bronco-bucking title. Now the steer-roping championship was in the balance. Four men were slated to compete in the finals: Ikua, Archie, Dickerson, and Hugh Clark, who a week earlier had taken second place at a rodeo in Encampment, Wyoming.

The Hawaiians had the fastest roping times so far, of 63 and 69 seconds. Dickerson was next with 71 seconds, and Clark in fourth place at 78 seconds. Any one of them could take the title with an outstanding showing in the final round.

Ikua went first. His peers would later say that as he stood perfectly still, waiting for the signal to ride, he looked like a statue of Kamehameha the Great. It was almost ten years to the day since the Hawaiian flag had been lowered over 'Iolani Palace and Hawaii had lost its independence. Now a paniolo had a shot at winning a contest that had become quintessentially American.

In that moment, the taciturn cowboy was an ocean away from the world he knew. The windswept prairie of Cheyenne, with its sense of endless space, must have been dizzyingly foreign to the islander. Yet he was also in his element. Chasing a steer—whether here, across the plains of Waimea, or down to the beach at Kawaihae—this was what he was born to do.

According to Purdy family lore, a rainbow appeared over the arena in Cheyenne just before Ikua's final ride. The rainbow, along with the shark and the wind, was an *aumakua* of the Purdys, a deified ancestor that watches over the family like a guardian angel. When Ikua saw it, he felt the calming presence of his forebears.

As the flag fell, Ikua launched his horse after the steer that was already tearing down the field, throwing its head to either side. He swung his lariat twice overhead and threw.

The loop took the steer around the horns. Ikua spurred his horse ahead, whipped the end of the rope around his saddle horn, and veered sharply to one side, snapping the noose tight. The thousand-pound steer slammed to the ground and lay stunned for a few seconds, its legs waving in the air.

As Ikua dismounted, one of his feet caught briefly in a stirrup, costing him valuable seconds. But his horse kept the rope tight as he sprinted to the prostrate animal. Six seconds after making the cast he had busted the steer to the ground. He whipped the piggin' string around its feet, tied the knot, and stepped back with his hands raised.

His time elicited gasps around the arena: 56 seconds flat, the fastest of the competition by more than 7 seconds. Ikua's average of less than a minute per steer made him the man to beat. In the words of one reporter, it would take "a sensational record performance" to overtake him.

Dickerson was next. His first cast slipped off the steer's horn. He busted the animal but it leapt up, then leapt up again, and soon "America's Hope" was out of the running.

Hugh Clark drew a real sprinter. The cowboy made a perfect throw and busted his target as quickly as Ikua had. For a moment it looked like he might have a chance. But the steer flailed powerfully as Clark tried to make the tie, thrashing all four feet until the last loop was around its heels. The clock kept ticking, and by the time Clark had finished it read 1:20.4. His average time was almost 20 seconds slower than Ikua's. In rodeo terms, an eternity.

The Hawaiians had clinched first place. The only remaining question was whether Archie could outdo Ikua.

Archie made a huge first throw and busted his animal in an astounding 36 seconds. But then he encountered the same problem as Clark, a steer that squirmed free. The paniolo had to hold the animal on the ground with brute force, and his tie ended up taking well over a minute.

Ikua Purdy—paniolo, Hawaiian, American—was the steer-roping champion of the world.

WHEN IT WAS TIME to present the steer-roping award, something had changed at Frontier Park. Although the title had gone to "a stranger, and one might almost say a foreigner," in the words of the *Wyoming Times*, the Hawaiians had won over the audience.

As rodeo officials gathered on the field to present Ikua with a new saddle and a prize of $240, a man in a U.S. cavalry uniform leapt from the grandstand and ran out to embrace the paniolo. Clarence Lyman, the first native Hawaiian to enroll at West Point, was so overcome with emotion that he couldn't resist the urge to shower his fellow islander with congratulations.

Archie's time put him in third place behind Clark, with Dickerson in fourth. Jack, despite his asthma attack, managed to place sixth.

Ikua waved and bowed to the roaring crowd. For the reserved cowboy, this was exuberance. Later he would tell his children and grandchildren that competing in "Waiomina" was an adventure. Winning was a joy, but that was about all he ever said before changing the subject or, more likely, riding off toward the mountain to chase more cattle.

15

GEMS OF THE SEA

E ho ʻi nā keiki ʻoki uaua o nā pali.
Home go the very tough lads of the hills.

WITHIN HOURS OF WINNING at Frontier Days, the paniolo were hit up with requests for a rematch. C.B. Irwin even put $400 on the table for a second chance. The Hawaiians passed and chose to start their journey home. Ikua and Archie took the Overland back to San Francisco and left for Hawaii aboard the *Alameda*. Jack and Emily stayed on the mainland for another week, visiting friends. They all left Cheyenne with a standing invitation to return, but none of them ever did.

The *Alameda* docked in Honolulu on September 11, 1908. Throngs greeted the ship as a band played "See the Conqu'ring Hero Comes," but the music was almost lost amid the jubilation. Ladies in their Sunday best rushed the gangway with leis for the returning heroes. A local poet stood on the landing, drafting verses of welcome:

> *Alas! for all those champions—*
> *From far across the sea,*

With face all tanned and steady hand,
To meet the best in all the land,
Came our Hawaiian Three.

Those who knew Ikua noticed that he had shaved off his trademark mustache. He told a reporter that the women of Cheyenne had been so crazy for souvenirs that "they took our leis, our belts, our chaps, our spurs and everything removable that they could find about us. So when more of them clamored for souvenirs I took off my mustache and gave them each one hair and, say, there was just enough to go round."

"Champion Roper and His Companions Are Home," blared the front page of the *Pacific Commercial Advertiser*. Below the headline was a photograph of Ikua and Archie draped in leis and seated stiffly in chairs, a debonair Eben Low standing behind them. In another paper, the joy of the occasion inspired still more poetry:

Purdy, the sturdy, we've heard he has won.
For the little old isles of Hawaii,
The world's roping contest, and what he has done
Is a plum in our promotion pie.

Kaʻauʻa took second, while sixth man was Low
In the steer-stringing stunt of the earth,
And it's up to the cow-catching artists to know
What our lariat laddies are worth.

Three cheers, then, for Purdy, and then just a few
For Archie and Jack, three times three!

The boys of Hawaii who gallantly threw
For the fame of these Gems of the Sea!

Eben had been traveling to Honolulu from the island of Kahoolawe when he first heard the results from Cheyenne. He beamed like a father: "I have good reason to feel proud," he told a reporter. Not only was he related to the victors, but it had been his idea in the first place to show the world that paniolo are as talented as any cowboy. His pride never faded in the years to come, and he made sure that Hawaiians understood his role in this narrative. He posed for photographs with the winners, and, in future retellings, made it sound like he had been there himself.

Two nights after the *Alameda* returned, Eben hosted a luau in Waikiki to celebrate. The guest list included well-to-do members of the business community and Jonah Kūhiō, a Hawaiian prince and delegate to the U.S. Congress. Toast after toast kept everyone's glasses full, and at one point Ikua was urged to speak. He gave "a very clever speech in Hawaiian," according to witnesses, with an extra helping of thanks to his cousin for making the whole Cheyenne endeavor possible.

Then it was Eben's turn. He announced that he was "no speech-maker," then, as one paper put it, "proceeded to disprove his assertion by making a wonderful verbal exposition of the work and methods of Purdy and Ka'au'a at Cheyenne." He waxed on about the training of young cowboys and, for the non-ranchers in the audience, detailed just how well the paniolo must have performed to beat the world's best. As for why he had chosen Ikua and Archie to represent Hawaii, he said:

I had watched them and trained them myself, and I
knew that they would never get rattled in a tight pinch.
I have watched them rope wild bulls on the mountain-
sides under conditions and difficulties that the plains-
men never saw, and I knew that they would stand the
test . . . I felt assured in my own mind that they would
keep themselves in the best of condition and would be
an honor to the Hawaiian Islands in every way. That,
gentlemen, is why I selected them, and just how right
my choice was you know now and all the world knows.

A few days later Ikua and Archie sailed home to Hawaii,
with a stop in Maui along the way. On both islands they disem-
barked to cheers, flowers, flags, and an outpouring of joy for
Hawaii's newest heroes. Throughout the islands, celebrations
continued for weeks.

ON THE MAINLAND, NEWS of the astonishing upset in Cheyenne ran
in papers from coast to coast. Perhaps inevitably, there was effort to minimize the Hawaiians' accomplishments. "Steer Lets
Kanaka Win," read one headline. "Had Clark contended with a
steer as docile as that of Ikua," a Cheyenne paper wrote, "it is
probable the championship would be still held by an American."

Many accounts mislabeled the paniolo as foreigners, showing how unclear mainlanders still were about the islands' political status. (Even a Hawaiian newspaper drew a distinction
between the paniolo and "the American boys.") Newspapers as
far away as upstate New York announced:

For the first time in the history of the Frontier Day sports at Cheyenne, the championship for steer roping has been taken away from the United States . . . This is tremendously important—more so, in fact, than the result of the Marathon race or winning the greater number of points in an Olympic contest. No one country has enjoyed a monopoly of the sport of foot-racing, pole jumping, hurdling, or tug-of-warring, but America did have a monopoly of wild horse riding, steer roping and all the sports and exercises in which the frontiersman and the cowboy took part. It is rather galling, therefore, to have this honor taken from us.

The article did at least conclude by calling the paniolo "natives of an island that is protected by the Stars and Stripes," but that hardly diminished the overall impression of a humiliating alien assault.

In response, the *Hawaiian Star* reprinted the offending piece under the title "Roping Glory Follows the Flag," with a cheeky postscript:

> *Since Hawaii's in the U.S.A., I cannot understand*
> *Why she thus should be referred to as a sort of foreign land;*
> *The lariat laurel still adorns a brow American*
> *In fair Hawaii, U.S.A., and Purdy is the man!*

Word of the paniolo's victory eventually made its way to the White House. Representative Kūhiō presented President Roosevelt with a letter and a picture of Ikua, and reported that the president was delighted by the news of the outcome in Cheyenne.

THE DRAMA IN 1908 couldn't have been better publicity for Frontier Days. If the paniolo had returned to compete the next year, they would have seen a three-way rematch between Clayton Danks, Dick Stanley, and Steamboat. Danks rode the famous bronco again, but nothing could top 1908's performance, in part because the judges had forbidden the use of spurs. Even though the audience called for "Stanley and Steamboat!" the Oregon cowboy drew a different horse. When the results were announced—Danks in first place, Stanley in sixth—the crowd started throwing cushions and howling "rotten!" and "robbery!"

The Stanley-Steamboat matchup was bittersweet for those who had fallen in love with the mighty horse. The bronco spent his twilight years in a Wild West show until 1914, when he had to be put down after an injury caused by running into barbed wire. The "grand old horse of the passing west" earned a seven-paragraph obituary in the *Daily Leader*, and is still remembered as one of America's all-time great bucking broncos.

Stanley was killed when a horse fell on him at a rodeo in 1910. But after his death, his story took an even stranger twist: Dick Stanley was in fact Earl Carl Shobe—and he was wanted for murder. Shobe had been part of a team of outlaws who ran in northern Wyoming in the early years of the twentieth century. He was linked to murders as far away as Chicago, prompting him to flee to the West Coast, grow a goatee, and assume the alias Dick Stanley.

But laying low wasn't in Shobe's character. In Oregon, he and his brother started the Stanley Bros. Congress of Rough Riders, and he became so confident in his new identity that he was willing to travel to Cheyenne and take center stage at Frontier Days, even though there was a $5,000 reward out for him.

For the sexual assault of his next-door neighbor, Pete Dickerson was arrested and was soon breaking rocks at the Wyoming State Penitentiary in Rawlins. Clayton Danks eventually quit rodeo and found work as a sheriff. He served as a Frontier Days judge and lived to ninety-one, irked to the end that he couldn't be inducted into the Rodeo Hall of Fame while he was still alive. "I considered shooting myself to get my name on the list," he joked.

None of these rodeo stars would have known such success had it not been for Buffalo Bill Cody, who died in 1917. His traveling show turned cattle-country skills into an enormously popular spectacle with worldwide appeal. Yet Cody did more than that: he helped shape, for better and for worse, the very concept of the Wild West, and by extension the myth of America itself.

If there was ever a single rodeo that challenged that myth, it was Cheyenne Frontier Days in 1908. Just as the binary conceits of the American West—cowboy versus Indian, civilization versus wilderness, good versus evil—were crystallizing in the national psyche, along came a small posse from afar whose story pushed back against such simplistic thinking.

At home in the islands, the paniolo triumph in Cheyenne was far more than a sports victory. Ikua, Archie, and Jack became the first superstars of twentieth-century Hawaii, the first heroes who weren't politicians or royalty. By winning in

Wyoming, the men had put the islands on the map and had shown the world what Hawaiians could accomplish. As the *Hawaiian Star* put it: "Now that they have seen a man from the Parker Ranch beat all their champions, they will realize that the Hawaiian Islands are something more than a hula platform in the mid-Pacific."

The win was something that "all Hawaiian hearts can be happy about, for the honor garnered by our boys," wrote another paper. Hawaiians were still grappling with the injustice of annexation and the cultural onslaught wrought by explorers bringing cattle, missionaries bearing Bibles, and foreign politicians exercising the breathtaking arrogance of imperialism. Ikua and his cousins hadn't set out to become a symbol for Hawaiian strength and identity in the new century, but that is exactly what they became.

IKUA PURDY NEVER LEFT Hawaii again. Back on Parker Ranch, he took the prize saddle he had won in Cheyenne, stuck it under his porch, and got back to work. As far as anyone can tell, he never used it, shrugging it off like he did the title of world champion. He still competed, though. On New Year's Day in 1909, at a rodeo event in Waimea, he bested Jack, Archie, and other locals by roping a steer in 47 seconds.

In 1918, drawn by an offer of higher pay in Kauai, Ikua left Parker Ranch. Two years later, he moved to Ulupalakua Ranch on Maui, where he worked alongside his friend and former rival Angus MacPhee.

Ikua and his family stayed at Ulupalakua for the next thirty years. The Purdys lived in a brown ranch-style house set in a grove of eucalyptus, beside which Ikua planted fragrant ilang-ilang trees. From the window of his tiny bedroom he looked out on cattle pastures and, in the distance, the Pacific Ocean. Across the street stood a small stone church and the cemetery where MacPhee would later be laid to rest in 1948.

On the mainland, the paniolo were virtually forgotten. But time only burnished their legacy in Hawaii. Ikua eventually stopped competing in rodeos, but continued to serve as a field judge and gave the occasional interview. By the 1930s, his story had begun to sound more like folklore: as one article put it, the world champion roper, still going strong at sixty-four, had been born "with the dust of the range, smoke of the branding fire in his nostrils."

Some details of the paniolo's story mutated over the years. Many people in Hawaii, including members of the Purdy family, came to believe that the trio's hosts in Cheyenne deliberately provided them with bad horses. The claim traced back to a 1909 article in the *Pacific Commercial Advertiser* that incorrectly stated Ikua had been given "an untried and poor horse." From other accounts and expert analysis of contemporary photographs, however, it's clear that the horses, when they did finally show up, were top-quality mounts.

For his part, Ikua was loath to boast about his unofficial role as "cowboy king of the islands." He once told his son and grandchildren, "I may have that title, but on Mauna Kea, there are so many cowboys like me."

Besides, if Hawaiians needed to celebrate local cowboys, they always had Eben Low. The self-appointed elder statesman of paniolo culture would fill that role for decades, tirelessly promoting Hawaii and himself. In 1909, Eben moved to Honolulu to run his salvage and shipping business. He also continued organizing annual parades, although he moved the date from July 4 to June 11—Kamehameha Day.

Eben also befriended, and at one point even tried to start a business with, Angus MacPhee. In a bizarre coincidence, MacPhee lost his left hand in a hunting accident on Parker Ranch in 1910. The two men competed every now and then in one-armed roping contests.

Just a few years after the adventure in Wyoming, Jack Low died of a brain aneurysm in the hamlet of Kukuihaele on the north side of Hawaii. He was fifty-four years old. In 1918, Archie Ka'ua'a was severely injured when he was struck in the chest—not by a horse or charging bull, but by the engine crank of a backfiring Ford Model T. He died soon after, only thirty-six years old.

A month before Archie's death, the Waimea Boys, minus Jack, had reunited for a rodeo contest at Kapi'olani Park in Honolulu. Organized by Eben and MacPhee, it was the first "real roundup" in years and included cowboys from all over. The media played it up, recalling the story of the celebrated paniolo of Parker Ranch who had vanquished the mainland's best.

In 1953, *The Honolulu Advertiser* ran an article marking Eben's eighty-ninth birthday, accompanied by a photograph of the old cowhand seated in a wheelchair. The paper described him as a "cowboy, sailor, cattle rancher, civic leader and affectionately known to early day paniolo as 'Rawhide Ben.'" Ebenezer Parker Kahekawaipunaokauaamaluihi Low passed away in 1954, aged ninety. His ashes were scattered near the summit of Mauna Kea.

In his twilight, Ikua took pleasure in watching his grandchildren learn to ride—saddle, bareback, it didn't matter as long as they were on a horse. Anyone was welcome in the Purdy home, but whenever conversation would drift toward the topic of Ikua's prowess, he would say something like "There are plenty of things to talk about besides me."

He died on July 4, 1945, at the age of seventy-two. Until his death he was still working cattle at Ulupalakua Ranch. He was survived by his wife, nine children, and three grandchildren.

Ikua was inducted into the National Cowboy & Western Heritage Museum's Rodeo Hall of Fame in 1999, ninety-one years after his triumph in Cheyenne. In one obituary, Eben Low was uncharacteristically brief: "No one was his equal." It was the tribute Ikua Purdy deserved. Not the best Hawaiian cowboy or the best roper in the islands. Just the best.

ON THE MOUNTAIN

No alien land in all the world has any deep, strong charm for me but that one . . . Other things leave me, but it abides; other things change, but it remains the same.

—MARK TWAIN, writing about Hawaii in 1889

JANUARY 2018: THREE PICKUP trucks wind their way up the reddish dirt road, flanked by barbed wire fence strung between bleached wooden posts. To the west, across the plains of Waimea, sunshine splashes the verdant slopes of the Kohala Mountains. To the east, grazing cattle dot rippling pastures and cinder cones. The snow-frosted summit of Mauna Kea floats in the background.

Much of this rangeland is still owned by the Parker Ranch, but Mānā Road—unpaved, rutted and rocky in sections, overgrown with thick grass in others—is open to the public. A mile or two back are the crumbling stone remains of Jack Purdy's island homestead. Up ahead lay the gravesites of John Palmer Parker and his descendants.

Our group for this weekend excursion consists of retired paniolo, two forest restoration experts, an archaeologist, and a few strays, including the two of us. The trek, which is really a drive mixed with walks and pit stops to "talk story," will take us up and across the northern flank of the volcano, past abandoned cowboy stations, stone paddocks, hidden caves, and other landmarks that animate the history of ranching on Hawaii.

At noon the trucks pull into the shade of a eucalyptus grove. About thirty curious cattle mill on the other side of a nearby gate. One of the cowboys opens a cooler and distributes chopsticks and plastic takeout containers of teriyaki chicken or beef with rice and steamed vegetables. Someone else unwraps a block of *haupia*, a coconut and taro dessert, which he cuts into slices with a pocket knife.

Everyone eats fast. The old-timers, hands tucked into the front pockets of their blue jeans, lean back against one of the trucks and chat about what the future holds for the paniolo way of life. Some residents of Hawaii, especially those who work or worked in the cattle industry, would like to see the Purdy home preserved and turned into a historic site of some kind or another. The idea is a prickly one, though. To some, honoring an Irish immigrant made famous by his work with animals brought here as objects of imperialism doesn't exactly qualify as preserving Hawaiian heritage.

As we stare out over the hillside, a seventy-four-year-old paniolo named Sonny says that there used to be so much more rain here, but in recent decades the climate has become drier, hotter. Climate change will affect Hawaii's coastline most dramatically, but it's also predicted to decrease trade winds, throwing rainfall patterns into confusion throughout the islands.

Since the heyday of ranching in Hawaii, higher and higher costs, combined with cheap production elsewhere, have squeezed the islands' cattle industry. Over the last half century, many ranches closed, consolidated, or morphed into operations blending horseback-riding tours and conservation. Nonetheless, the island of Hawaii still has tens of thousands of animals on its remaining ranches, and as many as 2,000 feral cattle continue to roam the high country.

Paniolo, on the other hand, are an endangered species. Most cattle management nowadays is done from the seat of an ATV. When it comes to professional cowboys, those who truly depend on horses for work, there are perhaps thirty left on the island, with maybe another two dozen on Maui.

Yet rodeo is as popular as ever. Contests and cowboy-themed celebrations run throughout the year and on all the major islands. Local rodeos include *po'o wai u*, an event unique to Hawaii, in which contestants race to tie a steer to a post, an echo of the technique once used to tire out feisty bullocks. Despite the small number of working ranches and the limited need for workaday cowboys, Hawaiian high schoolers frequently qualify for the National High School Finals Rodeo on the mainland, and local rodeo fans know the names of island stars like former bull-riding champion Myron Duarte, who won top honors at more than forty of the country's biggest competitions.

Meanwhile, Waimea is thriving. The city has a vibrant arts and theater scene, and schoolchildren study in Hawaiian-language immersion schools. Tourism is important, as it is throughout most of the state, although the cooler climate and dearth of beaches mean Waimea's sidewalks tend to have as many organic farmers and astronomers as they do sunscreened vacationers. (The W. M. Keck Observatory and Canada-France-Hawaii Telescope perched atop Mauna Kea both have their main offices here.)

And paniolo pride is everywhere. The annual Paniolo Parade held each September brings the town of 9,200 to a virtual standstill. Bands and singers march toward the city park, followed by a procession of exquisitely dressed paʻu riders. In the middle of town, the parade passes by the Parker Ranch Center, a pastel-colored shopping plaza with telltale vertical facades of Old West architecture and stop signs that read WHOA. In one corner of the parking lot stands a life-size statue of Ikua Purdy on horseback, about to fling his lasso toward a running steer.

ON THE SECOND DAY of the Mauna Kea adventure, the group stops to inspect old homesteads and bullock pits, learn about archaeological excavation sites, and witness firsthand the spread of gorse, a thorny, fast-growing, and invasive shrub that now covers huge swaths of mountainside. But in other areas, Mauna Kea's story is one of rejuvenation. A massive koa tree, for example, grows directly atop the stone foundation of a nineteenth-century cabin, while elsewhere seedlings of these mighty trees are now protected by fences so cattle can't get at them.

That night's camp is a rarely used cowboy cabin at about 6,000 feet, only a few miles from where Eben Low suffered his near-fatal injury in 1892. Soon after arrival, someone fires up the woodstove to heat water for the furo, the steel-walled tub just large enough for a person. In a shack filled with cut lumber, the small bath could double as a watering trough, but that doesn't make it any less inviting after a long day on the road—or in the saddle.

After sunset, a few members of our party don jackets and warm hats to sit outside by a fire and sip whiskey from red Solo cups. The old-timers, opting for warmth, crowd around the table in the kitchen near a blazing woodstove. One of them pulls out a weathered binder full of black-and-white photographs. In one image, a beaming Eben Low stands beside a young girl, probably a granddaughter, seated on a horse. Even for a quick family photo, Eben, always the showman, wore a holster and pistol.

Everyone nods in agreement about the lasting impact of the 1908 victory in Cheyenne. One experienced hand reiterates just how hard it is to loop a steer while riding downhill at full speed, let alone doing so from far away, and with a huge loop like Ikua used. A part-time paniolo, whose family still runs a ranch above Kailua-Kona, tells how cowboys visiting from the mainland will contact his family, hoping to join a cattle drive: "When they see the lava fields and the steep slope and forest, they're like, 'Yikes, we have to drive cattle thru *that*?'"

The older generation of paniolo continue their discussion, spreading a map over the table and recalling old Hawaiian names for specific cinder cones, hillsides, and outcroppings. At one point there is talk of a seasonal freshwater spring. The two young resource managers hang on every word, taking careful notes. In addition to rodeo and a proud heritage, this transfer of knowledge is another way that Hawaii's paniolo are passing the torch. The islands' cattlemen and -women are experienced stewards of the local environment, and their expertise is in-valuable to those whose job is to protect and maintain these lands for future generations.

After a while, though, it's time to close the binder and stop taking notes. The old-timers retire to their sleeping bags, while the rest of the group lingers beside the fire pit outside. Some-one pulls out a ukulele. While he strums and sings, sparks from the fire rise toward a sky made silver with stars.

ACKNOWLEDGMENTS

We are grateful for the support, encouragement, and faith of so many people. For research and reporting assistance, a special thank-you to author and longtime Parker Ranch veterinarian Billy Bergin, Momi Naughton at the North Hawaii Education and Research Center, Peter Mills at the University of Hawaii, Mike Kassel at the Cheyenne Frontier Days Old West Museum, and Sam Low. To Phyllis Edwards, sleuth extraordinaire: without your uncanny skills and irrepressible curiosity, this book would be a far lesser work. Thank you to Byrd Leavell at United Talent Agency for championing this project, and Peter Hubbard, our talented and tireless editor at HarperCollins.

We would also like to thank the staff at the following institutions: American Heritage Center at the University of Wyoming, Buffalo Bill Center of the West, Wyoming State Archives, Denver Public Library, Hawaii State Archives, Bishop Museum Archives, Kona Historical Society, Multnomah County Library, Stephen H. Hart Library and Research Center, and Tangipahoa Parish Library.

Chris Higgins, Jason Lathrop, and James Smith read and made helpful comments on early versions of the manuscript, and Nicola Pinson provided crucial insights and endless support.

Others who gave generously of their time and knowledge include Kala Lindsey Ah Sing, Daniel Akaka, Nick Amphlett, Kuʻulani Auld, Bill Bergin, Brady Bergin, Marie Bertellman, Carl "Soot" Bredhoff, Adam Burns, Kualiʻi Camara, Wally Camp, Mary Carver, Scott Craven, Leslie Dean, John Deeben, Colene De Mello, Tom Eschelman, Robin Everett, Dave Foreman, Marcie Greenwell, Nahua Guilloz, John Haines, Carla Hanchett, Molly Harris, Wayne Higa, Buddy Hirsig, Glena Hirsig, Tom Hirsig, Joy Holland, Faithy and Roy Horner, Jaidy Jardine, Sonny Keakealani Jr., Erik Klemetti, Philip Lewis, Matt Martin, Jodie Mattos, Rawls Moore, Jennifer Nelson, Andy Nordhoff, Susan Ozawa, Eric Page, Hannah Parris, Ron Powers, Parrish Purdy, Michael Purdy, Walter Ritte, Anthony Roberts, Christine Robertson, Greg Shine, Erik Steiner, David Swanson, Patrick Symmes, C. Kahanuola Tabor, Suzi Taylor, Mace Vaughan, Coert Voorhees, John Waggener, and Bill Woo.

To the rest of our friends, respective families, and readers everywhere: thank you for making it all worthwhile. Aloha.

SELECT BIBLIOGRAPHY

Ambrose, Stephen E. *Nothing Like It In the World: The Men Who Built the Transcontinental Railroad 1863–1869.* New York: Simon & Schuster, 2001.

Anderson, Sam. *Boom Town: The Fantastical Saga of Oklahoma City, Its Chaotic Founding, Its Apocalyptic Weather, Its Purloined Basketball Team, and the Dream of Becoming a World-Class Metropolis.* New York: Crown, 2018.

Barna, Benjamin Thomas. "Ethnogenesis of the Hawaiian Ranching Community: An Historical Archaeology of Tradition, Transnationalism, and *Pili.*" Ph.D. diss., University of Nevada, Reno, 2013.

Bartlett, Ichabod S., ed. *History of Wyoming.* Chicago: The S. J. Clarke Publishing Company, 1918.

Bergin, Billy. *Loyal to the Land: The Legendary Parker Ranch, 750–1950.* Honolulu: University of Hawaii Press, 2003.

Bergin, Billy, and Brady Bergin. *The Hawaiian Horse.* Honolulu: University of Hawaii Press, 2017.

Brown, Dee. *The Gentle Tamers: Women of the Old Wild West.* Lincoln, Nebr.: Bison Books, 1981.

Cassity, Michael. *Lives Worth Living, History Worth Preserving: A Brief History of Wyoming Homesteading, Ranching, and Farming,*

1860–1960. Cheyenne: Wyoming State Parks & Cultural Resources, 2010.

———. *Wyoming Will Be Your New Home . . .: Ranching, Farming, and Homesteading in Wyoming, 1860–1960*. Cheyenne: Wyoming State Parks & Cultural Resources, 2011.

Cody, William F. *An Autobiography of Buffalo Bill (Colonel W. F. Cody)*. New York: Cosmopolitan Book Corporation, 1920.

Cowan-Smith, Virginia, and Bonnie Domrose Stone. *Aloha Cowboy*. Honolulu: University of Hawaii Press, 1988.

Dabney, Eric, ed. *Historic Cheyenne: A History of the Magic City*. San Antonio, Tex.: HPN Books, 2006.

Davis, David B. "Ten-Gallon Hero." *American Quarterly* 6, no. 2 (Summer 1954): 111–125.

Federal Writers' Project. *The WPA Guide to California: The Golden State*. San Antonio, Tex.: Trinity University Press, 2013.

———. *The WPA Guide to Nevada: The Silver State*. San Antonio, Tex.: Trinity University Press, 2013.

———. *The WPA Guide to Utah: The Beehive State*. San Antonio, Tex.: Trinity University Press, 2013.

———. *The WPA Guide to Wyoming: The Cowboy State*. San Antonio, Tex.: Trinity University Press, 2013.

Fee, Art. "Steamboat, King of the Buckers," *Canadian Cattlemen*, Nov. 1965, pp. 12-13.

Fischer, John Ryan. *Cattle Colonialism: An Environmental History of the Conquest of California and Hawai'i*. Chapel Hill: University of North Carolina Press, 2015.

Fleming, Candace. *Presenting Buffalo Bill: The Man Who Invented the Wild West*. New York: Roaring Brook Press, 2016.

Flynn, Shirley E. *Let's Go! Let's Show! Let's Rodeo!: The History of*

Cheyenne Frontier Days. Bremerton, Wash.: Wigwam Publishing Company, 1996.

Gant, Harry Arthur. *I Saw Them Ride Away.* Castle Knob Publishing, 2009.

Hackler, Rhoda E., and Cummins E. Speakman. "Vancouver in Hawai'i." *Hawaiian Journal of History* 23 (1989): 31–38.

Haley, Evetts, ed. *Cowboys Who Rode Proudly.* Midland, Tex.: Nita Stewart Haley Memorial Library, 1992.

Hanesworth, Robert D. *Daddy of 'Em All: The Story of Cheyenne Frontier Days.* Cheyenne, Wyo.: Flintlock Publishing, 1967.

———. "Early History of Cheyenne 'Frontier Days' Show." *Annals of Wyoming* 12, no. 3 (July 1940): 199–212.

Hough, Richard. *Captain James Cook: A Biography.* New York: W. W. Norton & Company, 1997.

Hoy, James F. "The Origins and Originality of Rodeo." *Journal of the West* 18 (July 1978): 17–33.

Knowlton, Christopher. *Cattle Kingdom: The Hidden History of the Cowboy West.* New York: Houghton Mifflin Harcourt, 2017.

Larson, T. A. *History of Wyoming.* Lincoln: University of Nebraska Press, 1990.

LeCompte, Mary Lou. "Wild West Frontier Days, Roundups and Stampedes: Rodeo before There Was Rodeo." *Canadian Journal of History of Sport* 16, no. 2 (December 1965): 54–67.

Lyons, Curtis J. "Traces of Spanish Influence in the Hawaiian Islands." *Hawaiian Historical Society Papers of 1892.* Honolulu: Bulletin Publishing Company, 1904.

Mattison, Ray H. "The Hard Winter and the Range Cattle Business." *The Montana Magazine of History* 1, no. 4 (October 1951): 5–21.

May, Bill. "Two Champs." *Steamboat Magazine*, Summer/Fall 1991.

McMurtry, Larry. *The Colonel and Little Missie: Buffalo Bill, Annie Oakley, and the Beginnings of Superstardom in America*. New York: Simon & Schuster, 2006.

Mills, Peter R. *Hawai'i's Russian Adventure: A New Look at Old History*. Honolulu: University of Hawaii Press, 2002.

Mills, Peter R., Carolyn L. White, and Benjamin Barna. *Humu'ula: An Archaeological Perspective of Hawaiian Ranching and the Pacific Hide and Tallow Trade*. Unpublished draft, 2011.

———. "The Paradox of the 'Paniolo': An Archaeological Perspective of Hawaiian Ranching." *Historical Archaeology* 47, no. 2 (2013): 110–32.

Moulton, Candy. "Rodeo Flight School." *True West*, May 2, 2005.

National Railway Publication Company. *The Official Guide of the Railways and Steam Navigation Lines of the United States, Porto Rico, Canada, Mexico, and Cuba*. 1908.

Olmsted, Francis Allyn. *Incidents of a Whaling Voyage*. New York: D. Appleton and Co., 1841.

O'Neal, Bill. *Cheyenne: 1867 to 1903: A Biography of the "Magic City" of the Plains*. Fort Worth, Tex.: Eakin Press, 2006.

Porter, Willard H. *Who's Who in Rodeo*. Oklahoma City: Powder River Book Company, 1982.

Propst, Nell Brown. "A Foot in Each World." *True West*, June 1979.

Puakō Historical Society. *Puakō: An Affectionate History: The Life Story of a Small Community on the Island of Hawai'i*. Vancouver: Granville Island Publishing, 2000.

Rasenberger, Jim. *America, 1908: The Dawn of Flight, the Race to the Pole, the Invention of the Model T, and the Making of a Modern Nation.* New York: Simon & Schuster, 2007.

Richardson, Warren. "History of the First Frontier Days Celebrations." *Annals of Wyoming* 19, no. 1 (January 1947): 39–44.

———. Early Recollections of Old Cheyenne." *Cheyenne Chamber of Commerce Newsletter,* July 1951.

Riley, Glenda, and Richard W. Etulain, eds. *Wild Women of the Old West.* Golden, Colo.: Fulcrum Publishing, 2003.

Roberts, Phillip J., ed. *Wyoming Blue Book, Volume V.* Wyoming State Archives, State Parks and Cultural Resources Department, 2008.

Siddall, John W. *Men of Hawaii: Being a Biographical Reference Library, Complete and Authentic, of the Men of Note and Substantial Achievement in the Hawaiian Islands, Vol 2.* London: Forgotten Books, 2017.

Slatta, Richard W., Ku'ulani Auld, and Maile Melrose. "Kona: Cradle of Hawai'i's Paniolo." *Montana: The Magazine of Western History* 54, no. 2 (Summer 2004): 2–19.

Sodaro, Craig, and Randy Adams. *Frontier Spirit: The Story of Wyoming.* Boulder, Colo.: Johnson Books, 1996.

Stewart, Charles Samuel. *A Visit to the South Seas, in the U.S. Ship Vincennes: During the Years 1829 and 1830; With Scenes in Brazil, Peru, Manilla, the Cape of Good Hope, and St. Helena.* New York: J. P. Haven, 1831.

Thigpen, Jennifer. *Island Queens and Mission Wives: How Gender and Empire Remade Hawai'i's Pacific World.* Chapel Hill: University of North Carolina Press, 2014.

Thomas, Heidi M. *Cowgirl Up!: A History of Rodeo Women*. Guilford, Conn.: TwoDot, 2014.

Twain, Mark. *Mark Twain's Letters from Hawaii*. Edited by A. Grove Day. Honolulu: University of Hawaii Press, 1975.

Union Pacific Railroad Company and Southern Pacific Railroad Company. *The Overland Route to the Road of a Thousand Wonders*. Issued by the Union Pacific and Southern Pacific Passenger Departments, 1908.

Urbic, Momi. "Purdy Ranch: Home of Legendary Waimea Cowboy." *Historic Hawai'i News* 5 (January 1979): 6.

Van Sant, John E. *Pacific Pioneers: Japanese Journeys to America and Hawaii, 1850–80*. University of Illinois Press, 2000.

Wellmon, Bernard B. "The Parker Ranch: A History." Ph.D. diss., Texas Christian University, 1970.

Westermeier, Clifford P. *Man, Beast, Dust: The Story of Rodeo*. Lincoln, Nebr.: Bison Books, 2008.

Williams, Henry T. *The Pacific Tourist: Adams & Bishop's Illustrated Trans-continental Guide of Travel, from the Atlantic to the Pacific Ocean*. Edited by Frederick E. Shearer. New York: Adams & Bishop, 1884.

Writers' Program of the Work Projects Administration in the State of Wyoming. *Wyoming: A Guide to Its History, Highways, and People*. Lincoln, Nebr.: Bison Books, 1981.

Zwonitzer, Mark. *The Statesman and the Storyteller: John Hay, Mark Twain, and the Rise of American Imperialism*. Chapel Hill: Algonquin Books, 2016.

Among the hundreds of newspaper, magazine, and journal articles we drew from, some of the most useful came from: *Eve-*

ning Bulletin (Honolulu), *Honolulu Star-Bulletin, Honolulu Star-Advertiser, Honolulu Advertiser, Hawaiian Star, Hawaiian Journal of History, Pacific Commercial Advertiser, Hamakua Times, Laramie Boomerang, Cheyenne Daily Leader, Cheyenne Leader, Cheyenne Daily Sun-Leader, Wyoming Tribune Eagle, Rocky Mountain News, Billings Gazette, Denver Post, Denver Republican, Denver Times, Denver Daily News, Colorado Magazine, Frontier Times, Annals of Wyoming, Wyoming Tales and Trails, San Francisco Chronicle, San Francisco Call, New York Times, Leslie's Weekly,* and *Harper's Weekly.*

INDEX